The Black Girl in the Classroom

Theodore Timms
BS. Ed; MS. Ed

Published 2019 by Huge Jam Publishing
www.hugejam.com

Images are the author's own except for stock images used under
Adobe license. Cover images are © lassedesignen (main) and
WavebreakmediaMicro.

ISBN: 978-1911249344

DEDICATION

On behalf of her brother Anthony, her mother
Melba, and myself - this book is respectfully
dedicated to my daughter Lauren Denise Timms
and to all of the women in my life in the hope that
I may influence their lives for the better.

CONTENTS

ACKNOWLEDGMENTS

I wish to express my sincere gratitude to the Lord Almighty for giving me the strength to hold on and finish my book. I sincerely and respectfully want to thank my darling wife for nurturing our daughter and son. But for my wife I'm nothing. Lastly, I would like to thank all my students in my 30 years of education who gave me the experience of becoming a part of their lives.

FOREWORD

An understanding of the history of African American families, especially fathers, is needed for us both as teachers and as empathic human beings that we may better understand the pressures, dynamics and weight of contexts (both past and present) upon black girls and their social, academic and professional destinies.

I therefore make no apology for the research-heavy chapters that follow. Without the academic observations and findings that I have been pulling together over many years and am now about to share with you, the action points that are included for embedding into your teaching practice will just hang at the end of the book like well-intentioned but optional truisms. Call it a thoroughly holistic, rather than a wordy, approach!

Nobody exists in isolation. "No woman or man is an island," to slightly misquote John Donne. In order to understand the daughter or the father, we need to look to the mother and the son and the grandparent too. To this end, the chapters follow a logical pattern, beginning with the African American community, then moving inwards through family, parents, then more specifically mother, father and you, the teacher.

However, I have chosen to begin this guide with definitions of and research into 'self-esteem' and 'self-efficacy' as these are two crucial predictors of success that I, as a father and an educator, want to see maximized in every black schoolgirl right now. Much, maybe most, of what I share in this book will be applicable to boys as well as to girls, and some of it will apply to children of all ethnicities. Nevertheless, my research shows that the father-daughter dynamic is key within African American communities and, in the interests of countering historical marginalization and under-achievement, it is in the context of this dynamic that my chapters find their most value.

I hope you find the key points and key questions that follow each chapter helpful rather than patronizing! But if the latter, you might find solace in this anecdote: in a professional development meeting with fellow beginning teachers our mentor handed out some tasks. He told us who we were to share with, what the color codes meant, and how we weren't allowed to write on them etc. etc. As we received our sheets, we started to exchange glances that pretty much said: "Is this guy for real?" After it was all set up, he asked us if we'd been feeling a bit annoyed by it all. Then he laughed and explained, "But we do it to our students all the time!"

1. HER SELF-ESTEEM

Name me someone who doesn't thrive on good self-esteem! It's a basic requirement for success and happiness, and by 'success' I mean the unmitigated success that comes with reaching your full potential. There are, of course, degrees of success and not all ostensibly successful people are confident all of the time. By the same token, very few people ever actually reach their full potential.

As teachers it is our professional duty to ensure that each and every one of our students is building the self-esteem that will help them to reach their own individual versions of the stars. Sounds to you like a well-worn platitude? Well, please don't mistake 'stars' for 'old chestnuts'… it is only a platitude because it's true!

The trouble with familiar phrases is that the words become empty over time. Hence our use of the word 'cliché' as a pejorative, referring as it does to a hollow phrase. So, the first task of this chapter is to reinvigorate the term 'self-esteem.'

What Is Self-Esteem?

The Long Answer

Think about when else we might use the word 'esteem'. It will be in relation to how we look at and judge someone: "I hold her in very high esteem!" Esteem is always qualified as high or low, either directly with an adjective as in that example, or indirectly through nuance and context: "she has esteem issues." Nothing 'hollow' about that. On the contrary, being looked at and judged, being regarded well or badly, having opinions formed of you, is pretty fundamental and a big deal. Even more so when the person looking at you is YOU!

'Self' is another loaded word. Too often linked to egocentrism (consider the negativity of the word 'selfish') it's a concept that carries a lot of confusing baggage: especially for middle-graders and young adults who are still trying to work out who they are anyway. I say 'too often' not because I think that it's good for people to behave as though the world revolves around them, or for anyone to always be putting themselves first. It's just that any prolonged or internalized negation of 'the self' will have a flattening, literally depressing, effect. The will to survive, the will to power, self-efficacy, is what helps people to achieve great things and it does not exist without a positive sense of identity.

The Short Answer

Self-esteem is the way you look at yourself and how you judge what you see.

Why Is Self-Esteem Important?

What if you look at yourself and see a whole host of negatives? There are a number of responses to this question: a question that for many, and in particular for many black girls, is not hypothetical. Here's how a lack of self-esteem might exhibit in class.

1. You might not mix easily with others in social contexts, such as group work, feedback/plenary time, and lunch breaks
2. You might not approach the teacher for help for fear you're not important or liked enough to be worthy of someone's professional time
3. You might not complete, or even start, tasks because of your expectation of failure
4. Constructive feedback might be misconstrued by you as rejection or damning criticism
5. You might have low resilience, making you just give up on tasks too quickly
6. You'll see negatives rather than positives in everything
7. Your inability to make confident eye-contact might come across to teachers and peers as rude and aloof

8. You won't believe that your dreams could become realities: A grades, commendations, career choice, further education, future happiness, wealth, acceptance, inclusion, confidence, beauty, personal impact, creative achievements, relationships. This will impact your effort grades and personal career planning[1].

9. You might be sidelined or even bullied by others in the class setting

10. You might avoid school

11. You might exhibit challenging behavior

12. You might engage in substance abuse

All of these symptoms could put you 'at risk'. At risk of failure, at risk of being emotionally vulnerable (a 'people-pleaser', a target for grooming), at risk of self-harming, or simply at risk of being unnoticed and having life pass you by – a very private and understated tragedy. The list above could go on, too… Take another look at it, add your own ideas, and then work out for each point how you could, through your planning and interventions, work to offset these negative patterns.

---

[1] This overlaps with 'self-efficacy', see chapter 2

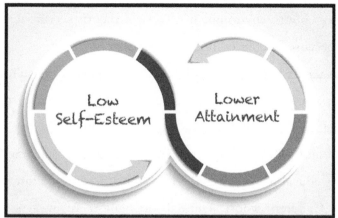

The vicious circle of low self-esteem

Self-Esteem: The Research

Research into self-esteem among black adolescents highlights some main themes that I'd like to share with you, some of which recur throughout this book. First, racial discrimination - which is itself tied in with the ever-present theme of power.

Racial Discrimination and Power

It's worth noting that degrees of racism have lurked behind or even driven some theories regarding self-esteem and success within African American families. For example, until the sixties the genetic model was prevalent, which argued that poor children of color inherited an intellectual inferiority. This model was replaced by the nurture-based belief that children of color fell short of achieving in school because they did not experience a cognitively stimulating home environment[2]. Today's theorists criticize these models because of their ethnocentric nature[3].

In his research, Delpit recognized the existence of a "culture of power" present in American classrooms[4], in which unarticulated values that reflected fundamental Anglo-American ideals were being practiced and promoted over the values of other groups. Schools and many educators expect children to conform to the culture of the school[5]. Children whose cultural orientation is in sync with mainstream ideals thereby become empowered in the classroom. Meanwhile, students whose cultural orientations are at odds with these ideals are placed at a disadvantage by classroom practices. This is because the cognition and behavior that has been critical to their self-understanding is being invalidated on a daily basis.

In the case of African American students, it is argued that disempowerment ensues when the non-mainstream values, behaviors and attitudes of black children are discouraged, ignored, or labeled 'inappropriate' for the school setting[6]. We will look more closely at what these non-mainstream behaviors and attitudes are in chapter four.

Also, it goes without saying that racism can also influence a child's self-esteem directly. Research has revealed that 96% of African Americans have experienced some type of racial discrimination in

---

[2] Bereiter and Engelmann; Deutsch et al
[3] Erickson
[4] Delpit
[5] Maxon
[6] Davis & Golden; Henry

the past year, 98% have experienced it in their life, and 95% report that racism is 'stressful'[7].

Next, we shall see that racism, including institutionalized racism, is also at work behind other factors that affect black girls' self-esteem, such as poverty and emotional development.

Emotional Development

Emotions are a complex set of behaviors produced in response to some external or internal event[8]. The theorist Banich uses a definition that describes emotion as "any strong feeling, such as joy, sorrow, reverence, hate, or love arising subjectively rather than through conscious mental effort"[9] and "agitation of the passions or sensibilities often involving physiological changes." Out of these definitions arise some of the most fundamental debates about the nature of emotion: are they rooted in mind or body? I think that I have a personal anecdote that might help illustrate this distinction.

I remember once a discussion in English class about the implications of Eve blushing in Milton's famous poem Paradise Lost. Some thought that the tell-tale blush was a sign of guilt – an emotion that Eve could only have felt through mental processing. Others saw the blush as a spontaneous, non-cerebral expression of innocence: a purely physical reaction to what was happening in the Garden of Eden. Neither argument won outright. I guess we could

---

[7] Klonoff & Landrine
[8] Bukatko & Daehler
[9] Banich

call it a dilemma of biblical proportions!

Why does it matter? Emotions are indelibly linked to self-esteem. If cognitive, self-esteem can also influence emotions back: a loop, a catch-22. "I feel inadequate so I can't do that right now." "My inability to do that has made me feel so inadequate."

> **Mind:** A number of scientists who study emotion have suggested that "relatively unconscious, but never the less cognitive, appraisals influence our emotional experiences, particularly our beliefs about ... the extent to which a circumstance furthers our goals"[10].

We have just discussed how cognition among students from less mainstream ethnic backgrounds can be dismissed, trampled on, invalidated by a 'white' traditional curriculum. So, we start to think how this disempowerment is going to feed into a student of color's ability to set and achieve her goals: in other words, how it will impact on her self-efficacy, especially if we accept that an individual's choice of occupation is to be viewed as an expression of their self-concept[11].

> **Body:** On the other hand, historical explanations, such as the James-Lange and Cannon-Bard theories, have centered on the role of physiological changes in emotion. For instance, the James-Lange theory argues that physiological responses to a stimulus cause the spontaneous onset of emotions.

---

[10] Banich
[11] Nawaz & Gilani

Mind & Body: The Cannon-Bard theory suggests that emotional states are influenced in equal measure by both physiological changes in the body and the processing of information by the brain. Other theories also vary in the importance they attach to functional (physiological) and cognitive (brain processing) perspectives of emotion.

Saami et al. describe emotion as a person's attempt or readiness to change the relation between themselves and the environment on matters of significance to them. However, placing emphasis on the consequence of an emotional state is argued to be a behavioral outcome. Emotion is more often described in terms of it being a subjective, psycho-physiological experience. For example, *Emotional Intelligence Theory* centers on the evolutionary path of human emotions. The primitive form of emotion served a "fight or flight" purpose[12]. But there is one advantage to emotions proceeding from thoughts… thought can impede human performance because it provokes emotions such as fear. Emotions can be turned to good effect if we teach our students how to manage them. Anger, for example, becomes a catalyst for courage to express concern about a misjustice, if it is managed so that it promotes persistence and prevents one from imposing physical or psychological harm. Rather than emotion being internalized and depressing, we should be looking to make it a constructive escape into proactivity and self-esteem.

This is called emotional adjustment and it is a prerequisite of

---

[12] Goleman

resilience and self-efficacy. Is emotional adjustment inherited, developed or both? While research since the nineties has suggested that it is in fact brainpower that sets the stage for emotional functioning[13], socio-environmental influences can have an impact[14]. So, we come back to racial discrimination. The social and political demands that a society places on its citizens and their respective communities can have a negative impact on family function. Specifically, parents experience obstacles if their historical or contemporary ideological values are perceived to be different. Reduced ability to adjust emotionally means less control, fewer positive outcomes, ever-reducing self-esteem and increased chances of being 'at risk'.

Socioeconomic Factors

Research has found that children who were at the lowest risk for behavior problems were exposed to fewer risk factors (e.g. income levels below the poverty line, lack of family support, mothers with relatively low levels of self-esteem and education/intelligence scores). Unfortunately for most of the students of color in our classrooms, the negative effects of racism impose color as a decisive factor in determining family poverty status[15]. Because low socioeconomic status affects so many variables within a family's

---

[13] Goleman; LeDoux
[14] Bronfrenbenner
[15] Horton et al.

microsystem[16] that contribute to development, impoverished African American children are placed at a higher risk for developing compromised ways of dealing with low self-esteem and negative emotions.

A recent study by Shakoor and Chalmers on the co-victimization of black youth in Chicago suggests that young African Americans are limited in their ability to discharge emotions by the socioeconomic conditions of impoverished areas. The consequences of poverty and other stressors tend to drive more adequate means of emotional expression underground, while drugs, alcohol and aggression become more prevalent substitutes. Without proper management (or adjustment) of emotions, emotional influences such as persistent fear, anxiety, lack of trust, impaired cognitive functioning, and lasting personality changes will persist[17].

Nurture

Past research has shown that females who were able to identify with and relate to their fathers had higher levels of self-esteem, independence and success[18]. Using these findings as a springboard, modern researchers now state that the father's influence affects not only academic performance but other aspects of his daughter's life[19]. During her adolescent years, if the father was present then the

---

[16] Bronfrenbenner
[17] Terr
[18] Baruch & Barnesst
[19] Boyd & Ashcraft

daughter was less likely to abuse alcohol and drugs. This research is considered later through chapters four to seven.

Chapter One Summary

Key Points

1. Everyone does better with high self-esteem.
2. Low self-esteem has a way of showing itself, so be aware of the signs.
3. Low self-esteem puts black girls 'at risk' in several ways.
4. Racial discrimination affects the self-esteem of black girls.
5. The traditional curriculum empowers white students.
6. Emotions are linked to self-esteem.
7. Even negative emotions can be managed to good effect: this is called 'emotional adjustment.'
8. Poverty impacts negatively on self-esteem.

Reflection Opportunities

- In chapter one there is a list of clues that a black female student might have low self-esteem. How can you address each of these 'symptoms'?
- Are there opportunities in your lesson plans for including learning that comes from African American culture? Even just one reference to a prominent African scientist/artist/writer/mathematician per lesson can have a cumulative positive effect
- Do you help your black female students to manage or redirect their emotions, or just stifle them?

2. HER SELF-EFFICACY

'*African American females with a high level of self-efficacy are better able to effectively develop and maintain skills to be assertive than females with a low level of self-efficacy. They are also able to be productive in the workplace despite barriers and obstacles.*' – Hackett & Byars

H mmm, strong stuff, this self-efficacy! But what is it?

What Does 'Self-Efficacy' Mean?

If something is efficacious, it means it's effective. Like Lily the Pink's medicine:

> *Let's drink a drink a drink*
> *To Lily the Pink the Pink the Pink*
> *The savior of the human race!*
> *For she invented medicinal compound –*
> *Most* efficacious, *in every case.*[20]

---

[20] Popular song in 1968 UK chart, by 'The Scaffold'

If your 'self' is 'efficacious', it's achieving... it's doing what it's meant to do. Things are getting better. Improving. Thriving. You're achieving, you're making great things happen. Just like your efficacious classroom and your efficacious lessons, I'm sure! Actually, it's even more than that, and it's deliberate that we looked at self-esteem first. Self-efficacy is a person's awareness of their ability to do these things. Clearly, if you have low self-esteem, your sense of your own efficacy will be affected. It will be a barrier to achieving future goals.

Self-Efficacy and Self-Image

In 2003, a researcher named Fabri assessed links between self-image and perceived self-efficacy during adolescence. His resulting article suggested that girls do better academically and can self-monitor; but when it comes to emotional self-efficacy their ability to self-monitor lessens. Also, Fabri's research found that girls experience higher levels of stress during adolescence[21]. A year later, research by Powell showed that girls have degrees of identity conflict and low self-esteem that can affect school success and healthy identity development[22]. The same research suggested that the father can have a positive impact on this; see chapter six.

---

[21] Fabri
[22] Powell

Barriers

In the extract quoted at the start of this chapter, Hackett and Byers mention those omnipresent barriers. We've talked about some of these barriers already in chapter one: things like racial discrimination, low self-esteem, an absent father, poverty. You don't want to be another (albeit unintentional) barrier, and you're reading this book because you'd rather be a metaphorical 'bridge' or some other form of conduit: an enabler and facilitator. You want to give all your students self-efficacy, and your black female students especially will benefit.

As educators we use goals and target-setting most every day, and we are both driven and judged by outcomes. What's going to be the outcome of this learning objective? How differentiated do the outcomes have to be for successful intervention and inclusivity? Goals and outcomes are key terms in something called Social Cognitive Theory.

Social Cognitive Theory (SCT): The Definition

Social Cognitive Theory states that self-efficacy, outcome expectations, and personal goals are key components that encourage an individual to pursue long-term goals and successfully perform tasks[23].

---

[23] Bandura

Social Cognitive Career Theory (SCCT)

Social cognitive career theory holds that not only are the actual events of an experience important, but the meaning attached to the experiences are too[24]. Social cognitive career theory connects career and social cognitive theory to examine how career and academic interests influence career choices and later become actions[25]. The theory suggests that these interests are primarily developed from self-efficacy and outcome expectations[26]. Many black girls dismiss what are in fact realistic career goals prematurely because of inaccurate self-efficacy and outcome expectations. Lack of self-belief can make any goal or idea seem unattainable[27].

On the other hand, all students are attracted to tasks that make them feel competent and successful. How can we stretch and challenge our students without compromising their sense of competence? By building their trust: showing them that we believe in them, that we're proud of their progress and admire who they are as people, being consistent in praising and rewarding them.

Outcome Expectations

In SCCT, outcome expectations refer to an individual's beliefs about

---

[24] Bandura
[25] Byars & Hackett
[26] Lent & Brown
[27] Albert & Luzzo

what is realistically likely to happen (as opposed to what the individual would like to happen). However, self-efficacy greatly affects outcome expectations. When an individual holds a strong interest in an activity, they will expect a positive outcome from it; if there is doubt that a positive outcome will result, an individual can quickly lose interest in completing the task.

The good news for us as teachers is that individuals are motivated by receiving rewards ('golden tickets', vouchers, stickers, merit points); pride (displayed work, principal's commendation, publication, applause) and self-respect (the actual process of completing the activity). Outcome expectations tend to have a greater influence than self-efficacy on engaging the interest of girls who are members of minority groups[28].

Personal Goals

Setting personal goals is the second tenet of SCCT. Goal-setting is a critical part of career planning and the development process; as such it contributes greatly to behavior – behavior being a key indicator of self-esteem levels.

When a student sets her own goals, it assists her with organizing, guiding, and sustaining her own behavior[29]. She will be able to implement her personal agency through those goals[30]. Self-efficacy - with its attendant outcome expectations - contributes to goal setting.

---

[28] Chronister & McWhirter
[29] Lent et al.
[30] Bandura

By association, self-esteem does too. NB: it is important not to confuse goals with attained skills[31].

Self-Efficacy and Career Choices: The Research

Behind much of the research that has been made into SC(C)T is the hope that the findings will be beneficial to all professionals, educators included, that work with African American females in developing and implementing evidence-based interventions and techniques. Interventions and techniques that are aimed at increasing levels of self-efficacy, career achievement, and aspirations among female African Americans.

Researchers Nawaz and Gilani conducted a study in 2011 to examine the relationship between parental and peer attachment bonds and self-efficacy in career decision-making among adolescents and post-adolescents. The study involved 300 males and 250 females from government colleges and from the universities of Rawalpindi and Islamabad, Pakistan. They discovered a positive relationship between parental and peer attachment and career decision-making self-efficacy. However, parental influence was greater than peer influence. Further research conducted in more 'individualistic' cultures shows that parents there do not intentionally attempt to influence their children's career achievement and aspirations.

---

[31] Byars & Hackett

However, they are a primary influence. Furthermore, they have a positive effect in safeguarding their children from community obstacles, including those listed in chapter one of this book. For more detailed discussions on how African American parents have an impact on their daughter's futures, see chapters three and seven.

Middle grade is a pivotal time to start studying and understanding the career development of women[32] and fortunately, over recent decades, there has been a significant growth in literature that focuses on women's career development[33]. However, a woman's career self-efficacy still is not equivalent to a man's career self-efficacy because of gender role socialization and its effect on career opportunity and range[34]. For all ethnicities, too many girls' beliefs about their future careers are affected by gender expectations. Women are also more likely to consult with others about their career options and be influenced by the opinions of others concerning career decision-making than men are[35].

The majority of African American women has always worked and has historically had higher labor force participation rates than white women. The task of participating in the workforce has caused African American women to exhibit stronger work ethics. African American women represent a significant sector of the US labor force; however, here's the rub: not much is known about their career development[36]. Historically, high-income jobs have been offered to

---

[32] Watson, Quatman & Elder
[33] Hite & McDonald
[34] Theran
[35] Li & Kerpelman
[36] Byars

individuals who were deemed stable upper- and middle-class citizens. Black women and men have always faced job discrimination and have not received the same employment opportunities as their white counterparts.

Barriers such as discrimination and gender-role socialization can play a major role in future planning for the African American girls in our classes. Their perception of such barriers affects their belief about their ability to succeed in the workforce. Such disbelief lowers their self-efficacy, causing them not to pursue certain occupations, career options, and advancements[37].

The risk is that such barriers will continue to significantly impair their ability to provide

economically for the well-being of their families and to advance in the workforce: *The John J. Heldrich Center of Workplace Development*[38] suggests that workplace environments are different for African Americans than for any other racial/ethnic minority group: African Americans are perceived to be most likely to be treated unfairly in terms of promotions and opportunities for training, and most likely to be discriminated against at work[39]. For African American girls, that's a double-whammy. No wonder we need to instill resilience and self-efficacy.

---

[37] Byars
[38] The John J. Heldrich Center of Workplace Development (2002)
[39] Combs

Chapter Two Summary

Key Points

1. Black girls with high self-efficacy can 'get things done' and are aware of the power they have to effect change.
2. Self-efficacy in black girls is linked to self-image.
3. During adolescence black females experience higher levels of stress than black males.
4. Social Cognitive Theory can help with setting goals.
5. Goals seem more achievable to black female students when they are praised and rewarded.
6. A black girl's 'outcome expectations' are what she believes can realistically happen.
7. A strong interest in a topic leads to higher outcome expectations, while low outcome expectations result in a lack of interest.
8. Goal-setting is a critical part of career-planning.
9. When black female students set their own goals, they become more organized, independent and motivated.
10. Gender expectations affect black girls' career choices.

Reflection Opportunities

- How can we stretch and challenge our students without compromising their sense of competence?
- How can we make 'outcome expectations' more ambitious?
- Which topics are most likely to interest your black female students?
- How often do your students set their own goals/targets?

3. HER HERITAGE

'but yu must come back tomorrow wid de whole of yu eye an de whole of yu
ear an de whole of yu mind an I will tell yu de other half of my story'
John Agard, 'Half-Caste'

John Agard is an English poet with dual heritage and the poem I quote from above is widely taught in the UK to 'middle-graders' and high school students. The anger detectable in his voice is a reaction to the ignorance of others in relation to his ethnicities. How can we understand and respect him if we don't understand his background?

With that in mind, this chapter has been written so that, should you yourself be from an ethnic background that isn't African American, you will have a better understanding of one more of those many diverse cultures that populate your classroom. And if you do have African origins (actually, modern anthropology thinks that all human beings have their very first roots in that great continent), well, here's a brief tour of your cultural heritage…

History

When North America saw the arrival of the first Africans, it also saw them being captured and traded as nothing more than commodities in what became known as the Transatlantic Slave Trade. More than twelve million Africans were shipped to this country in the seventeenth and eighteenth centuries. Slavery didn't just affect the economic wellbeing of African Americans. It took away their most basic human rights and from the very start we can see how racial discrimination and inequality became part and parcel of the American psyche and its legal systems. Ever since, African Americans have been fighting for equality and inclusion.

At the time of the Civil War in 1861, there were over four million African American slaves. I am using the modern term African American, but of course they would not have been considered to have American citizenship during their slavery. Although they had been resisting in various ways, often with European American help (sabotage, education, escape) it wasn't until this time that they saw a real opportunity for freedom. From 1861 to Lincoln finally signing the Emancipation Proclamation in 1863, thousands of slaves had already escaped and fled. During those two years they were often referred to as "contraband" since they were neither free nor enslaved. Just one of the many "limbos" that non-white ethnic groups still too often find themselves in even today.

In 1865, there was the end to the civil war and a decade ensued where the primary focus was the Reconstruction of America. One priority was to give equality to African Americans and one early result was the 13th Amendment that outlawed slavery.

1865   The 13th Amendment abolished the legality of the slave trade

1868   The 14th Amendment gave anyone born in the US automatic citizenship and reaffirmed its intention to give legal protection to all its citizens

1870   The 15th Amendment enfranchised citizens regardless of race

But things weren't as great as those new amendments suggested. From 1877 onwards decision-making and jurisdiction was defederalized and it was down to individual states to pick and choose their own laws. Segregation became commonplace and black citizens were kept away from polling stations. This was the terrifyingly violent age of the KKK. African Americans, especially those in the south, feared for their lives every day.

Many moved north. They worked hard wherever they found employment. Because they were still effectively barred from full civic participation, African Americans came to realize that they needed to attain a degree of financial independence or self-sufficiency and also attempt to strengthen and energize their communities through a kind of social and financial propaganda. Born in Louisiana at the time of the 14th Amendment was a woman who can stand as a role model to our black female students in the twenty-first century.

She was born Sarah Breedlove but after her marriage to Charles Walker became known as Madam C J Walker. Her impact went far beyond the fact that she built up an incredibly successful business empire selling beauty products. If you stand at a particular intersection in Indianapolis, you will see a four-story building adorned with African masks: the Madam C J Walker Building. Sadly, Madam Walker died at the age of 51 before the building was completed, but it stands as a reference to the cutting-edge training and scholarship program she provided for her 3000 female African American employees. Dubbed "Walker Agents," these working black women were able to gain financial independence. At her death she left behind $10,000,000[40].

Stamp showing Madam C J Walker. Released January 22nd, 1998, Indianapolis

---

[40] www.nps.gov/walker

Two world wars followed, and African Americans fought for the Allies. It was a natural development from that, many having laid down their lives for democracy, that the struggle for black equality should have felt re-energized. There followed a number of marches and demonstrations at what can be considered the beginning of the Civil Rights Movement. A movement that ended in 1965, on paper at least, when Johnson signed the Voting Rights Act: but not before attacks on peaceful protesters in Alabama had been broadcast. In terms of the education system, it was during this time that 21 states at last took the decision to desegregate America's public schools.

The Culture of Communalism

It's parents' evening! In the rare breaks you get between appointments you can people-watch. (Actually, you'll probably be marking or planning, but go with it...) Some parents look rather smartly dressed, possibly you're their first stop after the work commute; others are in jeans, tees, leisure-wear. Some look a little nervous (bad memories of their own school days?), some couldn't look more gracious and grateful; a few of them look like they're mentally preparing to go in to battle (did Ms. Davies really put little innocent Daniel in a detention last week for that?). One parent; both parents. Hey... hang on... that's a veritable group over there with Caroline Adebowale.

It sounds like a stereotype - and it is - but in this case, like a cliché, it's based on a (generalized) cultural truth. Traditional African American families do a lot of sharing, and this is often evidenced in communal nurturing, or extended families. So, don't hold back if you're talking to Caroline's older brother or her aunt, you are speaking to the right person.

Communalism is a black cultural value that places a premium on sharing; mutual aid; caring for others; interdependence; solidarity; reciprocal obligation and social harmony. When one's orientation is communal, human and spiritual relationships hold internalized meaning and value. Research has found communalism to correlate positively with emotions in African American children[41]. Communalism facilitates the emotional development of such characteristics as compassion, and attachment. Coupled with having adequate support and resources, the experience of being raised in a nurturing and communal environment facilitates secure bonding and preparation to deal successfully with stress later in life[42]. Research supports the concept that cultural values shape the social interactions of black families and influence the emotional development of black children.

Communalism: The Research

Communalism is defined as an awareness of the fundamental interdependence of people. It has often been cited as a family

---

[41] Jagers
[42] Mattis et al.

attribute of West African origin that produces interactive qualities such as helpfulness, empathy and affection[43]. So much so that one researcher, Jagers, has linked the emotional competencies it nurtures as a "communal morality"[44] that exists within the African American community. Communal values prescribe a morality of care that places priority on cultivating mutually-promoting relationships[45]. Application of this concept in the African American community comes out of a tradition of sensitivity and responsiveness to the needs of others. In his 1994 work, Blake suggests that the communication process between African American mothers and their children places a strong emphasis on interpersonal and emotional themes[46].

Interconnectedness, or communalism, is an intricate aspect of black cultural tradition that contributes to social forms of expression for many African American children. It is argued that black children like to feel connected to their caregivers, peers and teachers and are motivated to trust or cooperate through this connection. The connection helps them to achieve expected goals when they are working in conjunction with peers and teachers with whom they have bonded. There is also believed to be a predictive relationship between the practice of communalism in the home and academic achievement. It's likely that this can be explained by the positive effect communalism has on students' emotional competencies.

---

[43] Boykin; Greenfield; Jagers; Kochanska
[44] Jagers
[45] Gilligan
[46] Blake

The cultural factor of communalism has been shown to play a role in the black student's educational experience. Extended family members are instrumental in monitoring homework and class assignments, which subsequently keep the family up-to-date with the curriculum and their child's strengths and weaknesses[47]. As a result of extended family networks, parents are more effective teachers at home [48]. Sharing is promoted because it affirms the importance of social interconnectedness[49]. Empirical investigations by Boykin and associates have shown that communalism is a part of the capital that African American students bring to the classroom[50]. Furthermore, and of particular interest to educators, it has been demonstrated that black children achieve best within a communal context[51]. Black student performance can be enhanced by modifying the learning structure to include communalism. I hypothesize that nurturing parenting, academic involvement and endorsement of communalism will strengthen African American children's emotional adjustment. In turn, academic achievement levels will be positively affected.

Numerous studies have investigated relationships between family processes and socio-emotional competencies. Fewer have focused on links between black family processes and achievement. Those that have demonstrate the impact of financial hardship and other risk factors upon African American parenting and child adjustment[52]. There are complex socio-economic factors affecting

---

[47] John et al.
[48] Slaughter & Epps
[49] Boykin
[50] Ibid.
[51] Albury
[52] Luster & McAdoo

the ability of many African American families to continue with this traditional communal model, and those factors and their effects are discussed in chapter four.

African American Aspirations

In 2009, Spera, Wentzel and Matto conducted a study examining parental aspirations for children's education attainment in relation to ethnicity, parental education, children's academic performance, and parental perceptions of the quality and climate of their children's school[53]. The sample consisted of 13,577 parents of middle and high school students from large public schools in a mid-Atlantic state. Of the sample, 67.2% were Caucasian, 9.4% African American, 11.3% Asian American, and 5.5% Hispanic. Findings from this study revealed that over four-fifths of the parents across ethnic categories (86.9% African American, 88.3% Hispanic, 94.6% Caucasian, and 96.0% Asian) wanted their child to obtain a college or graduate level degree. This study suggested that Caucasian parents with lower levels of education had considerably lower education aspirations for their children than did other parents of other ethnicities with comparable low levels of education[54]. Overall findings of this study showed that parental aspirations for children's education were most predictive of non-Caucasian parents.

There are several studies focusing on parents' influence on

---

[53] Spera et al.
[54] Ibid.

children's educational expectations and attainment among African Americans. Studies that have generally found that African American parents' encouragement, support, and high expectations positively influence educational goals and attainment[55]. Since the early 1960s, behavioral and social scientists have given strong consideration to the role that black families play in the academic success of African American students. Black families are both credited with and criticized for the academic outcomes of their children. However, they have been recognized for utilizing education effectively so as to create opportunities to improve their place in life[56]. For more than a century a commitment to succeeding in school has been demonstrated by African American students. With the help of their families, African American children have made measurable gains in areas such as school enrollment and academic performance[57].

Church

Along with strong family networks, parents of high achieving African American students tend to indicate when asked a greater involvement in church-related activities[58]. Church involvement gives the parents an enhanced sense of control over their fate in life. Historically the Church, especially Christian Methodist and Baptist churches, have played a powerful role in black history in America.

---

[55] Trusty
[56] Billingsly
[57] Chideya; Billingsly
[58] Hidalgo

Martin Luther King Jr. was of course first and foremost a preacher. Churches would often host, or be the gathering places, for demonstrators and activists. As such, they continued to be active in politics (mainly on the Republican side).

Simple interior of Baptist church, Tennessee

After 1865 many 'black churches' were set up by African Americans, who then actively sought to move from predominantly white churches: a kind of elective segregation. Maybe it's the links with politics that have led to African American Christians being most associated with charismatic worship. After all, oratory is crucial when trying to effect social change. A decade later, as the spread of the KKK led to the displacement of many black families from the south to the north, huge churches (up to a thousand members) sprang up in urban areas.

Although Baptists were cautious about education, sensing that it took away from the instinctive, spiritual passion of its preachers, Methodists by contrast have been associated with facilitating the education of black emancipated families through Sunday schools and other offerings. So, many of your African American students will have moral guidance not just from the expansive nurturing of communalism, but also from today's church and from the legacy of church-involvement in political and human rights. For some African American students, both maternal and paternal socialization messages about African American history or racial pride is predictive of their achieving better grades[59].

---

[59] Brown, Linver, Evans, & DeGennaro

Chapter Three Summary

Key Points

1. Racial discrimination and inequality date back to the slave trade.
2. The end of slavery was followed not by better life-chances for African Americans, but by segregation and the rise of the KKK.
3. The black community became more cohesive and self-identifying after WW2.
4. 'Communalism' is a black cultural value that involves sharing and extended parenting.
5. 'Communalism' is linked to a positive 'communal morality.'
6. The Christian church figures largely in many black girls' upbringings.

Reflection Opportunities

- How do you show your awareness of black history in your teaching?
- Does your familiarity of the concept of the KKK make you underestimate or forget at times the horror of that period?
- Can you make use of communalism as a driving force towards higher achievement by engaging in conversations about your students' relatives? (Maybe, as with a few more of these suggestions, do the same with all ethnicities in the classroom rather than risk appearing to be singling out African Americans or responding to stereotypes!)
- Do you ensure that your black female students are contributing fully to SMSC (social, moral, spiritual, cultural) debates and discussions?
- How do you yourself model high moral conduct?

4. HER FAMILY

The previous chapter emphasized the communal nature of many traditional African American communities. Little surprise then that in just as many cases the family is more important to and influential within our black students' lives than it can be in the lives of children from more individualistic cultures. That's pretty much a summary right there! This chapter is, therefore, focused on the research that will help teachers to understand the powers at play in their black female students' homes. For the more specific investigation into the role of the African American father you will need to look at chapter seven (and chapter six for the mother's role). But the givens or donnés that form the framework for those chapters are introduced right here.

What the Research Tells Us

School Involvement

Resilience and family support have been proved to be two factors that contribute to the success of all high-achieving students[60]. Parent

---

[60] Herbert

and family practices cultivate life values in children through repetitive examples and lessons that are demonstrated throughout their developmental years. Internalizing and utilizing such values can have a positive effect on success in adverse school environments. Components that lend themselves to a successful learning environment include emotion-related characteristics that enable a balance of such cognitive skills as attentiveness and engagement with responsiveness and expression of opinions and comments. Parenting and family practices may also play a role in developing resilience that a black girl needs when having to demonstrate her capabilities in the face of detractors or under the burden of low self-esteem.

Positive gains in a child's academic and cognitive outcomes through parents' involvement can be seen as early as preschool[61]. Parenting practices central to ethnic minority families such as ethnic and racial socialization further influence the child's performance and outcomes[62]. When examining parental aspirations and their influence on children's career achievement and aspirations, it was discovered that parental ethnicity and education are important factors to consider. African American parents place a high value on education and report significantly higher career aspirations for their children than Caucasian parents[63]. On the other hand, as we have mentioned elsewhere, socioeconomic status influences parental involvement among minority parents. Many do not have the income due to low

---

[61] Arnold et al.
[62] Benerjee, Harrell, & Johnson
[63] Spera, Wentzel, & Matto

wage shift work to support the need of books, learning supplies, and educational experiences outside of the classroom. The work schedules of minority parents tend to be more rigid, leaving little time at the end of the day for them to provide attention to their children's homework[64]. Something to bear in mind when setting and marking homework, and when issuing or requesting the purchasing of core and revision texts.

Finally, let's look at how important it is for the child to see the parents' involvement. Notable descriptions of parent involvement define it as a function of commitment, time, and resources.

Pulkkinen suggests that involvement should be thought of in terms of the effort put into child oriented versus other activities[65], and Grolnick and Slowiaczek define this as the dedication of resources by the parent to the child within school and extra-curricular pursuits[66]. The term 'resources' applies to the enhancement of a child's educational experience that results from resources established by the parents' involvement in the school and at home. It is recognized that differences in factors such as values, time commitments, and availability of resources impact how and where parents are able to devote their time and energy in involvement. Grolnick and Slowiaczek conceptualized three categories of involvement across familial domains - behavioral, personal, and cognitive/intellectual. Children experience resources by way of parents' behavioral involvement, which include actions

---

[64] Rank; Waldfogel
[65] Pulkkinen
[66] Grolnick & Slowiaczek

such as going to the school and participating in parent-teacher conferences or open houses. Personal involvement creates a resource of affective experience for the child. It demonstrates how much the parent values and cares about school and enjoys sharing school activities and interactions. Sadly, economics plays a part in how optimized a parent's time-commitment can be.

Career Prospects

It was Blustein, Prezioso and Schultheiss that discovered that attachment relationships strongly influence an individual's career decision-making process and the effects of insecure relationships limit an individual's ability to explore career choices without being fearful or anxious[67]. Since then studies have been conducted to identify cultural influences on career self-efficacy.

However, such studies have failed to explore racial and ethnic differences entirely or have only examined simple racial and ethnic differences[68]. When looking at a family and the components thereof it is important to identify the roles that exist within it. The different family roles can assist the professional in understanding what the family does and how its members interact with each other[69].

In 1987, a researcher named Helwig piloted a study that sought to determine if career aspirations and expectations changed from childhood to adulthood. This study involved a total of 208 second

---

[67] Perrone et al.
[68] Hackett & Byars
[69] Eshleman & Bulcroft

grade students that were interviewed every two years until they entered their senior year of high school to track changes in their occupational aspirations. Researchers in this study also compared three generations (students, parents and grandparents) within the same family to determine what roles family, parents (and teachers) play in a child's career development process[70].

The second graders were chosen from four different elementary schools in a Denver suburb. Full-time and part-time employment was reported by 90% of the fathers and 60% of the mothers and 43% actually had jobs identified as professional, technical and managerial. They were then re-interviewed in the 4th, 6th, 8th, 10th, and 12th grades.

Five years then passed and 103 of the original 208 participated in the last interview, of which only 35 (then aged 23 years) completed a 4-page career survey. The results indicated that 63% of the children in the study were currently single and five participants had children of their own. 31 participants earned incomes less than $40,000 and two reported incomes that ranged between $50,000 and $60,000. When individuals were asked, "what influenced you in high school regarding your career and educational achievements?" many participants identified their parents as their primary influence. Some participants went so far as to distinguish which parent was the most influential: 20 participants named their mother, and five named their father. The remaining participants named their teachers as the primary influence.

---

[70] Helwig

Regarding the cross-generational findings, Helwig demonstrated that types of employment differed between the three different generations due to the changes of occupational opportunities. Primary influence during high school years also caused a change in career aspirations over the years. Educational barriers in many of the families prevented opportunities for certain types of employment. Researchers further noted the importance of the school counselors and administration working with the parents to provide tools and techniques so that they can be of assistance to the child's career development.

In African American culture, family plays a major role in career achievement, and this study agreed with more race-focused research that demonstrated that the main role model for African American girls is their mother[71]. Limited research has been done on the involvement of African American fathers with their daughters, hence my initial motivation for writing this book.

The roles of mothers and fathers are both influential factors in the daughters' career aspirations; however, their respective roles in the process are different. A black girl's high degree of closeness with a parent might pose an obstacle to her pursuing a career that differs from her parents' choice. Females need the support and closeness from their parents, but they also need to be able to pursue their own ideas and beliefs in regard to their career goals. Separateness empowers a student to be more independent[72]. In this regard, a

---

[71] Hackett & Byars
[72] Li & Kerpelman

mother should be aware of her influence on her daughters' life and use that influence in a positive manner to support the daughters' career aspirations. Fathers should be mindful of the authority they hold with their daughter and encourage her to express separateness, but within a supportive father-daughter relationship[73].

Economics

In the United States, it is common for the mother to have a lower income and occupational status than the father. DeVaney and Hughey reported in 2002 that African American women are the most disadvantaged population in the American workforce[74], and this may be due to gendered career selections. More than half of African American women are employed in low-paying and less secure jobs[75], and it is thus important to gain an understanding of the social factors that led to those career choices.

Some recent research by Garg and associates made an alarming observation, one that certainly justifies my book's titular phrase "at-risk black girls." Career expectations of adolescent males are influenced by their ability, academic achievement, and opportunity, whereas career expectations of adolescent females are influenced by socioeconomic status and parental expectations[76].

Low income black families face special challenges because of

---

[73] Ibid.
[74] Devaney & Hughey
[75] Booth & Myers
[76] Garg, Melanson & Levin

economic stress and disparities in education[77]. Economic stress has an indirect effect on the quality of parenting, making it difficult for single and two-parent (or caregiver) families to resolve conflict. The conflict impedes parents' nurturing and level of involvement with their children. Lack of both can have a negative effect on a child's positivity, school behavior, and academic achievement. At the heart of educational disparity are differing profiles of the schools that serve low income African American and other communities.

Schools in communities with social and economic privilege attract and retain experienced and talented administrators and teachers. Such communities also have more schools that maintain high standards and expectations of achievement for their students. Despite the need for high standards of recruitment and expectations in achievement across communities, something we are all of us working towards, it remains a fact that the combination of such characteristics is more difficult to obtain for school districts that serve low-income African American students. Traditional research suggests that families bear the responsibility for adopting practices that prepare a student for classroom success. Such research fails to recognize or highlight the importance of the school's role in helping parents to assist children in ways that improve their performance[78].

In addition to the overwhelming problems that exist in the low-income sector of the black community, race-related complications can also impose complexities on the lives of African Americans who

---

[77] Conger et al.; McLoyd; Brody
[78] Epstein

are middle-income earners. While historical attempts at resolving race discrimination resulted in civil rights legislation that has helped black families to improve their standards of living, new challenges also arose[79]. These challenges have affected traditional ways that black families rear their children and have developed social/community networks.

To illustrate, consider the three products of the civil rights movement- school integration, Affirmative Action, and equal housing laws, and the impact that they have had on the lives of African Americans. To some degree, each has served to provide access to better employment, education, and housing opportunities for African American families.

However, all three resources rarely exist within the same community. As a result, African American families with limited income must choose to live close to one, but rarely all three, of the following: schools with goals of high achievement, neighbors who can relate to or respect their cultural heritage, or jobs with adequate salaries and respectable commutes. Optimizing advantages in each area imposes time-consuming triangular logistics.

Families travel to work, school, and home, often times in different directions, with little or no community connection between the three places. This has impacted social resources that have traditionally contributed to those all-important communal strengths within the African American community. Relationships are not as established with neighbors and family, and children have less time

---

[79] Brookes

for rest, relaxation, or neighborhood bonding in the presence of caring adults.

In addition, children's requests to participate in school activities and socialize with classmates outside of school go unfulfilled because those responsible for getting them back and forth, the parents, are overwhelmed. (Consider Pulkkinen's research on parents' school involvement - see two sections above - in the light of these facts.)

Parents

The argument above is supported by an interesting piece of research by Yan who used Coleman's social capital theory[80] to show that low-income families of successful African American students demonstrate equal or higher levels of parental involvement via social capital than do those of successful European American students. What makes it interesting is that in order to conduct the research, Yan divided the capital four groups: (1) parent-teen; (2) parent-school; (3) parent-parent and (4) family nouns. Parental involvement via social capital was higher in all but one of the four groups[81]... the only group that was not higher was parent-parent, suggesting the erosion of communalism.

---

[80] Coleman
[81] Yan

'SOCIAL CAPITAL THEORY'

Social groups and networks that allow a person to achieve more with others than they could on their own.

The increased stress associated with attempting to balance the time-consuming journeys involved in work/school commutes and social events affects the emotional development of black children because of the impact on their parents' emotional energy. In addition to the quality of a parent's child-rearing skill, the ability to implement skills is facilitated by the ease with which parents are able to meet the needs of their family within broader, ecological contexts.

While African American parents continue to encounter difficulties with finding adequate employment, pay, and even basic housing in stable neighborhoods with high achieving schools they are not given fair opportunities for advancement. Black employees are not able to move around in the job market as easily as white employees, which leaves them more vulnerable to company lay-offs, salary freezes, inaccurate appraisals, and lack-luster job assignments.

Factors such as the absence of local institutions that support upward mobility (i.e., employment companies and high achieving schools) and equal opportunities for equitable wages affect parents' emotional availability to their children. This despite the fact that we have already discussed how important family life is within the African American community.

Other research notes some positives. Many African Americans

are creative and resourceful in their efforts to develop successful child rearing strategies, engaging their children in pedagogical dialogues and consistent problem-solving tasks[82]. Van Tassel-Baska discusses how successful African American parents hold high expectations for their children and are sensitive to their accomplishments. Independence and self-confidence are instilled in their children[83].

Delpit suggests that African American parents are significantly more likely to use direct language such as, "Girl get your behind in the bathtub" instead of statements like, "Isn't it time for your bath?"[84]

In addition, Slaughter and Epps describe the African American preschool children who are academic achievers as children with mothers who set clear and consistent standards of behavior, but who *also are willing to consider the child's point of view*[85]. Parents of academically successful African American students appear to have stronger family networks or extended family support[86].

Moreover, parents of high-achieving African American students have greater interactions with their children. The interactions often include an authoritative parenting style, independence, structure, and consistent emotional support[87].

---

[82] Clark
[83] Van Tassel-Baska
[84] Delpit
[85] Slaughter & Epps
[86] Higalgo
[87] Shade

The Family Unit

Let's talk circles: Bronfrenbenner's circles. The African American family has been through a metamorphosis of changes and definitions. Social scientists have contended that African American families may be presented best by using an ecological approach.

The favored ecological approach was developed by Urie Bronfrenbenner in the mid-1970's. He devised a way of conceptualizing the family structure and how it works within the perimeters of the social, the cultural, the economic and the political. He visualized four spheres[88]. In fact, these spheres are limited for our purposes in that they are considered to be derived from Western ideas of the family (including the public image of 'fatherhood') that are still being perpetuated through various media and other institutional outlets, including schools. Later, Jennifer Hamer, with her slightly different take on the definition of a family (especially in relation to race and fatherhood) expanded and modified Bronfrenbenner's definition.

First, Bronfrenbenner's spheres, which are concentric circles labeled as follows:

1. microsystem
2. mesosystem
3. exosystem
4. macrosystem

---

[88] Bronfrenbenner

Bronfrenbenner's Circles

1. A microsystem is defined as a pattern of activities, roles, and interpersonal relations experienced by the developing person (e.g. child) in a given setting, experienced through particular physical and material characteristics. It's a term for how children interact. The examples he uses are the home, daycare center, playground, and so on. These example settings are what he terms the building blocks of the microsystem.

2. The mesosystem has two or more settings in which the developing person actively participates. The example he uses with regards to adults are the relations with their family, work, and social life. It is a system of microsystems. These systems are formed when a person moves into a different environment.

3. An exosystem refers to one or more settings that do not involve the developing person as an active participant, but which can nonetheless affect them as a non-participant. For example, a child may include their parents' place of work in her exosystem.

4. A macrosystem is a national system. In an example, he states that within a macrosystem such as France, a classroom, park, or school may look like and function much like another - but all differ from their counterparts in the United States.

Despite Bronfrenbenner's reference to the differences between macrosystems, one could say that Hamer felt that his circles were as ethnocentric as they were concentric! In 2001 she therefore modified the systems[89]. She, too, defines the exosystem as being comprised of one or more settings. But she refers to a setting that the father may never enter - but in which events occur that affect what happens in all environments. For instance, Hamer states that in this system the economy affects how a father will behave. This includes education, the labor force and the family arrangement.

Hamer suggests that micro, meso, and exosystem all work in concert to influence a father's paternal attitude and behaviors, forming a complex relationship between father and environment. Furthermore, Hamer states that a people's belief systems, ideology, and culture combine to form the prevailing environmental

---

[89] Hamer

conditions and beliefs about fatherhood and the family. She examines the larger social context in which contemporary parenting practices have emerged in which discussion are organized around the confluence of racist state policy, social and economic injustice, distorted media images, and Western notions of parenting. In addition, in her book, Hamer talks about the historical development of the black family from slavery to the present.

So, between these two authors we are given definitions of the family that put its origins in perspective from the beginning to the present, which can be used to give current researchers a picture of what's missing or out of balance.

The US census defines a family as two or more individuals that reside in the same household who are related by birth, marriage, or adoption. A household is a housing unit shared by individuals either related or unrelated. The composition of a family varies depending on an individual's social, political, economic, and cultural influences (remember those circles?). The family's economic status greatly affects their values and beliefs, lifestyles, networks, expectations and environment[90].

When looking at different families and their components it is important to observe and recognize the roles within the family. The different family roles can assist one with understanding what the family does and how they interact with each other. When applying the different roles of a *dysfunctional* family[91] it is important to

---

[90] Eshleman & Bulcroft
[91] Ibid.

understand that it is possible that family dynamics will change with changing circumstances, influencing many members of the family to adopt new family roles.

The percentage of African American children residing with both parents declined from 59% in 1970 to only 33% by 1994, and those living with only their mother due to divorce or separation increased from 21% to 22%. Statistics show that African American children are more likely than white children to reside in a single mother household[92]. The majority of births in the African American community are to unwed mothers and fathers and more than half of African American children will grow up in a fatherless home[93]. Absent fathers are blamed for the increasing poverty and welfare dependency among African American children and single mothers. However, there are factors that can impede the father's involvement with their child such as the father's relationship with the mother, availability of time, and residential distance[94]. (See the above section on 'Economics.')

---

[92] Hines
[93] Baytop
[94] Hamer

Chapter Four Summary

Key Points

1. Family support contributes to academic success.
2. African American parents place importance on their daughters' academic success.
3. Demanding work patterns leave African American parents less time and energy to help with homework.
4. Economics plays a part in how optimized a black parent's time-commitment can be.
5. The mother, followed by the father, is the biggest influencing factor on African American girls' academic and career aspirations.
6. School counselors help by providing black parents with the tools and techniques they need.
7. African American social networks, despite their importance to the culture, are breaking down under economic pressures.
8. African American parents tend to use direct language more than their white counterparts.
9. The black family unit does not have a simple definition.
10. Family roles change with changing circumstances (eg. divorce)

Reflection Opportunities

- How often do you communicate with African American parents, other than at scheduled conferences?
- Can you offer support with homework to black girls whose home set up might not be conducive to parents helping with homework?
- Do you 'signpost' homework tasks so that students can be more self-reliant?
- If a set task involves a child's family, can you provide an alternative task, just in case Mom and Dad are exhausted or at work?
- Can you adapt your language to suit your students' ethnic expectations/experience? Especially when giving feedback or instructions.
- Are you mindful of the fact that some students might be experiencing changes at home?

5. HER MOTHER

Have you heard the theory that women are good at multi-tasking? I can think of a number of cartoons and illustrations I've seen where a mother in smart business wear is (for instance) stirring a pan with one hand, fixing something with the other hand, and rocking a baby chair with a foot – probably while telling her husband on a hands free cell that he's forgotten to do x, y or z. I often wonder whether this isn't some kind of male propaganda that gets men 'off the hook' when it comes to doing too many things. 'Just admire how capable women are and feign ineptitude for an easier life!' But, rightly or wrongly, African American mothers are the epitome of this vision. American women generally have worked throughout the history of the United States, and have a historical legacy of being self-reliant, strong and financially independent[95].

One cultural characteristic of African American mothers is their ability to maintain multiple roles within the family. They manage multiple roles of caring for their home and family while working. In African American culture, preservation of multiple roles within the family has great meaning and is a long-established trend in African American culture for women due to the high number of single-

---

[95] Hackett & Byars

mother homes[96].

Most African American women learn that they must work in order to survive. They know from experience that they are not likely to get married to the father of their children[97]: Jennifer Hamer in her research into the family unit showed that African American men are less likely to marry the mother of their children than Caucasian men are[98]. A linked fact is that, unlike the African American mother, maintaining dual roles is a relatively new trend for the white mother[99]. It seems that African American mothers prepare for this dual role expectation by exposing their daughters to more non-traditional gender roles than do non-African American mothers, leading to them being less likely to have a problem with maintaining dual roles in the future[100].

There is a paradox here. Black women, probably as a result of their hard work and resilience, are known for their strength. However, it has been found that African American women prefer jobs that serve others[101]. Happily, as the work force has grown in general for women, so has the socioeconomic status of black people, thus giving black women more opportunities of taking up professional positions or even the option of staying at home[102].

Another paradox to be found as one juggles the huge amount of research that has been carried out on women and motherhood in

---

[96] Booth & Myers
[97] Hackett & Byars
[98] Hamer & Marcdhioro
[99] Booth & Myers
[100] Hackett & Byars
[101] Booth & Myers
[102] Herring & Wilson-Sadberry

African American communities is that, while researchers like Hackett & Byars have highlighted how black daughters are exposed to roles that are non-traditional, they themselves, together with others, argue that African American mothers are trapped in traditional domestic roles.

Occupational ranges in which African American women are employed have always been limited. The majority of working women are employed in traditional female occupations; however, African American women are overrepresented in traditional occupations[103]. They have frequently had to pursue employment choices that many feminists would consider "captives in the household" roles, which have usually been the unattractive jobs[104].

Once in the workplace, racial and gender biases cause inequities that saturate the daily experiences of African American women as they attempt to demonstrate and inquire about career advancement opportunities[105]. Race and gender are two important aspects of identity for the African American woman[106], both of which are and have been targets of oppression and discrimination here and abroad[107]. This composite of race and gender hinders outcome expectations.

The manner in which the barriers are dealt with by the mother are especially important as research has shown that the African American mother serves as the main role model to her daughter and

---

[103] Byars
[104] Percheski
[105] Combs
[106] Williams & Wiggins
[107] Szymanski & Stewart

that the modeling effects are high due to the maternal bond, gender, and cultural and class relevance. The mother's educational level significantly influences self-esteem, achievement, and self-efficacy for her African American daughter[108].

Much of this will be so familiar and research on the subject so easy to come by. What we know less about is the impact of the father on his daughter. While the mother's influence seems, on the whole to be a positive one, especially given the upward trend in career opportunities – a positivity mitigated by her expectation of a heavy workload and much domesticity – how is her influence added to or subtracted from by the modern African American father?

---

[108] Hackett & Byars; Mandara, Murray, Telesford, Varner, & Richman

Chapter Five Summary

Key Points

- Black mothers often have multiple roles within the family unit.
- Experience and black history have taught these mothers that they need a strong work ethic to survive.
- African American mothers often opt for workplace roles that see them serving others.
- Mothers are black girls' main role models.
- A black girl's self-efficacy can be connected to the employment level of her mother.

Reflection Opportunities

- Are there opportunities in your lesson planning to include case studies of successful women in traditionally male spheres?
- Can you encourage black female students to talk a bit more about their fathers in class discussions, rather than depend upon their knowledge of their mothers?
- Are there ways in which you can inspire girls with thoughts about careers that are not stereotypically female or 'black'?

6. HER FATHER

It is important to understand the relationship and influence of the African American father concerning his daughter and her level of self-efficacy, career achievement, and aspirations. Having awareness of paternal influences and their impact will allow both you, her teacher, and her father to assist the daughter with establishing culturally appropriate goals, expectations, decision-making skills, and implementation of her career plans. Increasing her perspective and awareness of the influences of her father will further enhance her ability understand and improve her level of self-efficacy in regard to advancing her career achievements and aspirations.

But understanding the role of the father in modern African American families is a challenge simply because not enough research has been done in this area. We know how important the mother-daughter bond is thanks to research, and the daughter is aware of the importance of her mother too. Their closeness can be a self-conscious factor in the daughter's outcome expectations and her general wish to please her mom. If over time the importance of the role of the father in a black girl's life can become common knowledge, a given, too then the motivators in the girl's life will have increased. Furthermore, the positives that the father will bring to that dynamic will complement rather than duplicate the those of the mother.

Even the most entry-level research on the subject demonstrates that the topic is worth far deeper investigation than it has hitherto received. In a study on African American girls aged between 13 and 28 years old a relationship was found between perceived closeness with their father and high grades and occupational aspirations[109]. Another study in 2003 found that girls who have less contact with their father and have had conflictive father involvement had extensive depressive symptoms, delinquent behavior, and school problems[110]. Mori suggested that supportive father involvement is associated with high self-esteem among females[111]. In spite of the results from these studies, however, there are still gaps in the literature. There is a lack of research applying *Social Cognitive Career Theory* (SCCT) to examine the relationship between perceived and desired paternal involvement of the African American father and its influence on levels of self-efficacy, career achievement, and aspirations of his daughter.

A good proportion of the studies that do exist tend to focus on dysfunctional relationships; for instance, Hamer's focus on the absent father. Just as children achieve more when they feel confident and appreciated, and while we absolutely admire and support the single mothers who juggle stresses and manage to nurture at the same time, it's interesting to bear in mind that men are more likely

---

[109] Hanson
[110] Coley
[111] Mori

to be good fathers if they feel important and included. Parents of both sexes were once children who either developed, or failed to develop, high self-esteem. Our need to be cared for and wanted doesn't stop once we enter adulthood: this applies to men and women equally.

Research has another gaping chasm: an overview of the dynamics of a single group, the African American middle school girls without the influence of fathers. Specifically, how a father can be the architect for building an African American girl's perception of self, an impetus for creating competitive educational achievement in middle school years among other peers, and the guiding hand for their positive socialization and decision-making during formative school years.

Barriers

History

Due to the troubled history of African Americans in general, African American men enter fatherhood at a marked disadvantage to fathers of other racial backgrounds. Therefore, the father and his ability to rear his children are hindered. Also, Hamer has written in her recent research that slavery, the Civil War, and the reconstruction period all forced African American fatherhood to be negotiated within social, economic, and political institutions that were not guided by a social contract, but by systems attempting to sustain black people at a cheap labor source[112]. Her research states that, "beginning with slavery, which lasted from 1654 until 1865, African American fathers were frequently sold away and separated from their children, as well as denied legal rights and responsibilities to their children."[113] In other words, the system set the African American family up for failure.

In spite of the struggles, Hamer indicates that when the African American father plays an active role in the lives of his children, that active involvement in the family structure can result in positive social, behavioral, cognitive, and academic outcomes. Unfortunately, many African American families struggle with a one parent matriarchal household, and the likely consequence is that African Americans have been remarkably underrepresented as students in higher education, both historically and at present[114]. A comment that suggests the father's involvement powers academic achievement.

Stereotypes

The history of the father in America has taken on many roles. An examination of Nielsen's research suggests that social science research can be misused and misinterpreted. This in turn can lead to false beliefs and damaging stereotypes[115]. Best states that it has been

---

[112] Hamer
[113] Ibid.
[114] Ibid.
[115] Nielsen

said that "bad statistics are harder to kill then a vampire." A memorable way to point out that it is hard to kill a popular belief even when there is no evidence to support it."[116] In effect, research is asking these questions: how do false beliefs, myths, misconceptions and stereotypes about fathers get started and how are they perpetuated? How do they damage or limit father-daughter relationships? And what are the myths and misperceptions that will do the most damage?

Nielsen even asks this question: Are fathers necessary? She goes on to answer... given the cost of raising children in our country, few people would disagree that fathers are necessary – financially. Men know that society expect them to provide for their children financially. Furthermore, Americans have traditionally believed and continue to believe that the father is the bread winner. Accordingly, there has been a limited emphasis on the role of the father in the child's development, especially with regard to educational outcome. *The focus of most research on the African American father has been his role as a financial contributor, leaving considerations of emotional and psychological contributions to those of the mother*[117].

Perceptions and Media

Wiemann and associates cite a book entitled *Black Fathers; An Invisible Presence in America*. The African American male has been described

---

as absent, missing, nonresidential, noncustodial, unavailable, non-married, irresponsible, and immature[118]. The authors state that these studies mean that African American men enter fatherhood at a distinct disadvantage and that the African American father has been discriminated against in America for hundreds of years.

Throughout history, African American men have been treated unfairly and have been portrayed as lazy, ruthless, evil and less than human and really have contributed nothing to society. In research African American male has been represented in psychological research as largely absent members of the African American family structure and these negative beliefs are deeply embedded in the mind of society. Some research goes even further, stating that negative stereotypes of African American men have been pictured in society as sexual predators who will abandon their family[119]. Therefore, this image has been ingrained in the consciousness of the public. In children's books, mothers are portrayed as nurturing twice as often as fathers are. 65% of children books show mothers exclusively taking care of the children[120]. Nielsen states that in all the Caldecott award-winning books from 1938 to 2002, fathers generally (of all ethnicities) were not involved in the rearing of children. Devlin states that there are an alarming number of movies depicting fathers as idiots; acting as fools while being manipulated by their intelligent daughters[121]. Nielsen and Rome suggest that television and movies

---

[118] Connor & White
[119] Smith, Krohn, Chu & Best
[120] Anderson, Kohler & Letiecq
[121] Devlin

'do a great job' of perpetuating negative stereotypes of African American fathers. These images consist of them appearing as criminals, rappers, athletes, or violent people[122]. Fathers are being portrayed as dysfunctional, with a distant and awkward relationship between themselves and their daughters[123].

In the same way that divorcing parents are advised to be respectful to and about one another in front of their children, it's important that children do not witness the denigration of their father (or either parent.) Perceived failings on the part of a parent become internalized and owned by the child, affecting self-esteem. Even where a father is absent because of incarceration, for instance, the child still needs to feel that love and respect for a man who has given her half her genetic make-up.

Data

Each night four out of ten children go to sleep without a father who lives in the home[124]. Lerman also states that fatherhood in America may be the weakest link in the family chain. The research again supports a commonly-held view that the nation's families are falling apart. The then Commissioner of Education, Horn, stated in an interview several decades ago that nearly 23 million children were not living with their biological fathers, and 40% of the children whose parents were divorced had not seen their fathers in the past

---

[122] Nielsen; Rome
[123] Stetz
[124] Lerman

year. These figures have increased year on year. He also suggested that there was no question that father-absence had reached epidemic proportions.

The Other Side...

Bryant and Zimmerman found that non-residential African American fathers usually reside in closer proximity to their children and visit their children more frequently than non-residential fathers of other races[125]. Though many African American fathers do not reside in the same home, African American adolescents reporting having closer relationships with their fathers than Caucasian adolescents. Adding such important information to current research can help take account of the parental involvement of non-residential African American fathers who are actively involved in their child's life but whose commitment is overlooked[126].

Studies have found that male role models play an extremely important role in the lives of young African Americans and two thirds of this group reported that they viewed their father as their male role model[127]. Studies have begun to examine both the physical and psychological presence of the father. Although the physical presence is an important component of psychological presence, the child is less likely to consider that factor when determining the

---

[125] Bryant & Zimmerman
[126] Hammond et al.
[127] Zimmerman, Salem & Maton

closeness of their father. A father can be physically present and psychologically absent[128].

In a 2009 book, Teachman shed light on the social and biological fathers who make positive contributions to the lives of African American children. It counters the negative labels typically attributed to black fathers in social science and popular literature with poignant examples of black men who are actively engaged in the lives of their families. The book's first chapter makes the important distinction between biological and social fathering and notes that the social science literature often ignores the efforts of many black men engaged in *social fathering*. Social fathering is the African American male such as uncle, grandfather, brother, or civic leader taking the place of the father when the biological father is absent[129].

---

[128] Thomas et al.
[129] Teachman

Social vs Biological Fathering

Coley (2003) conducted a study to increase the knowledge base on father-daughter relationships in African American families. The study consisted of 302 low-income African American adolescent girls from Chicago. Sixty-five percent identified a primary father; two thirds were biological fathers and one third were social fathers.

The study focused on how girls identified with their fathers and described their psychological attachment relationships. Girls who had less contact with their father and a conflictive father-daughter relationship had more depressive symptoms, delinquent behavior, and school problems. However, there was little relationship observed between father-daughter attachment and the adolescent girls' psycho-social well-being. In fact, results revealed that school difficulties escalated, with greater levels of anger and alienation, in the father-daughter relationship only with girls who identified with their biological father.

Outcomes of this study show a larger contribution of urban men in the lives of their children than is generally acknowledged. However, results from this study correspondingly raise concerns about the accessibility and effects of fathers in adolescent girls' lives. This concern is reason enough for researchers to discover and generate greater understanding on fathers' roles in African American families.

Single Fathers

The same Coles study focused on factors that enable and motivate single African American fathers to take full custody of one or more of their children. The number of African American single-father households has increased over the past three decades. Due to the rarity of single fathers, it is believed that they receive more sympathy and support from family and friends.

Results showed that the numerical number of single African American fathers is still increasing[130].

Relationships

Krampe and Newton examined the relationship between the fathers' presence in both African American and European American families and any reported feelings of closeness to the father figure on the part of the adult children of these families. They attained a participant sample of 650 individuals from four cities which were located in four different geographical regions of the United States. 454 of the participants were Caucasian, 196 were African American, and the average age of participants was 35 years old. This study included social fathers.

The research proved that African American fathers visited their

---

[130] Coles

children more frequently than the Caucasian fathers. In addition, the research shows that the African American children living with only the mother were closer to their fathers than were Caucasian children with the same family structure[131].

A study of 1330 children (boys and girls) showed that fathers who were involved on a personal level with their child's schooling, increased the likelihood of their child's success in academic achievements. When fathers assumed a positive role in their child's education, students reported feeling a positive impact[132].

Adolescence is the most difficult period for all children, and it is especially trying for girls if the father is not involved[133]. Also, daughters whose fathers promote their self-confidence and self-reliance during adolescence are more successful academically in college than girls with more protective or negligent fathers. If a father stresses the importance of independence his daughter is more likely to exhibit self-confidence and self-reliance than girls whose fathers are over-protective[134].

Fathers are very influential in determining the success of their daughters. Nielsen states that fathers who help their daughters establish a sense of endeavor excitement and agency in early childhood make them more likely to be successful academically and vocationally sound.

---

[131] Krampe & Newton
[132] McBride, Schoppe-Sullivan & Ho
[133] Nielsen
[134] Mori

Summary

It is imperative to continue to expand research on the African American father-daughter relationship and its influence on career achievement and aspirations. This will provide authentication for the development of counseling interventions and techniques geared at increasing levels of self-efficacy, career achievement, and aspirations among African American females in school.

Chapter Six Summary

Key Points

1. Much less is known about the black father-daughter dynamic than about the black mother's role.
2. Father-absence has been seen to be a contributing factor to black girls' depression, poor classroom behavior and low self-esteem.
3. African American men will be better and more active fathers if they feel involved.
4. Black fathers are victims of media and social stereotyping.
5. The 'usefulness' of an African American father centers around the financial support he can offer.
6. Even children's books minimize the presence and importance of the African American father (and fathers of all ethnicities).
7. A father doesn't have to live in the African American home to have a close tie with his daughter.
8. 'Social fathering' is common in black families where a male relative or church leader will take on the biological role.
9. There is a growing number of black single fathers.
10. A black father often has a positive impact on his daughter's sense of independence – this has been shown to increase achievement.

Reflection Opportunities

- If you mention fathers, should you mention 'father figures' too, as an alternative to help some students feel less marginalized?
- Have you used books that under represent the role of the father?
- Would your department/faculty head consider letting you add books and programs to resources that are more modern and inclusive in content?
- Do you tend to say: 'I'll contact your mother?' more than 'I'll contact your father' when home needs to be involved? (Always check student records first, never make assumptions about their home situations.)

7. HER CHILDHOOD

S omething that Saint Loyola (or Aristotle) didn't quite say... but almost did! In other words, our early childhood years really can determine who we turn out to be. Your middle-graders are in part who they are because of what they experienced before they even entered the pre-school gates. That doesn't absolve you... they are still developing: else what would be the point of this book, if it were all too late? But it does help to know that – just maybe – Caroline isn't working harder than Alicia because she's kinder or smarter, but because Alicia the toddler didn't quite develop the self-esteem that Caroline the toddler did.

We know from Maslow (what beginning teacher the world over hasn't dutifully filed away a handout of a colored pyramid: Maslow's hierarchy of needs?) that learning can only happen when basic nurturing needs are being met. The extent to which these needs are

---

[135] "Give me the child until he is seven and I will show you the man." (Atribution contested.)

met depends on factors such as family income, the father (or mother) being absent/present, comfortable housing, parental stressors, access to health clinics, social interactions, the giving or withholding of love, and so on. The first concern, however, has to be – does the child feel safe?

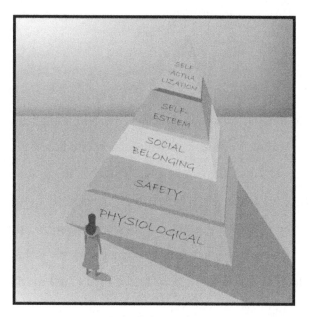

Maslow's Pyramid

Attachment Theory

John Bowlby developed attachment theory over 50 years ago. He defines attachment theory as an attempt to show the importance of security in promoting child development, personality development, and the affect (or emotion) regulation. This theory assumes that maternal sensitivity, responsiveness, and attunement are major factors in the quality of a child's attachment to her mother or 'attachment figure'[136].

<hr />

THE AFFECT REGULATION HYPOTHESIS

How individuals deal with any strong emotions, such as types of depression.

<hr />

This suggests that other, nearly-equal, component is the caregiver's own mental representation of attachment, her or his own internal working model experiences, developed in infancy and childhood[137]. Attachment theory presupposes that the need for closeness to the caregiver is an evolutionary biological necessity. Therefore, Bowlby states, attachment behavior must exist and be reciprocated for the young child to survive both physically and mentally[138]. This need for attachment continues on into adulthood[139]. Some things really do last "from the cradle to the grave."

Bowlby believed that thinking about children through the

---

[136] Ainsworth
[137] Harris
[138] Bowlby
[139] Ainsworth; Bowlby

framework of his theory helps us to understand a child's relationship to her mother and disruption of that relationship through separation, deprivation, and bereavement[140]. Ainsworth found that the theory contributed to the belief that the 'attachment figure' provides a secure base from which an infant can explore the world around her[141]. All connected research suggests that humans are social beings who seek connections with others. Also, research suggests that secure attachment between the parent and child plays an important role in shaping the child's development.

~~~~~~

AFFECTIVE

Emotional

~~~~~~

Studies have established associations between positive emotions and the existence of secure attachments between child and caregiver[142]. Attachment is an "affective bond" implying "strong emotions not merely security, anxiety, fear, and anger, but also love, grief, jealousy, and indeed the whole spectrum of emotions and feelings"[143]. An early attachment between African American children and their caregivers is an important emotional variable and carries

---

[140] Bowlby
[141] Ainsworth et al.
[142] Waters et al.; Gaensbauer et al.
[143] Ainsworth

characteristics similar to those described in the culture of communalism[144].

Culture

If culture is perceived as a set of beliefs, values and symbols that represent the worldviews held in common by its members[145], then practices will emerge out of those beliefs that will be unique to that group. With some exceptions, children's beliefs and behaviors will develop within the context of the group's worldviews[146]. Because time does not easily compromise ideology, cultural values influence children's development across generations, even among diasporas whose ancestors originated from a central region.

Some scholars argue that cultural influences take place very early in life and can have profound effects on the development of the preverbal child[147].

One of the ways that culture influences childrearing is through the caregivers' selection of interventions for regulating social signaling. The different styles of interactions raise fundamental questions about the nature of human emotions and the forces that guide emotional development. External or environmental situations produce distinct emotional reactions and behaviors that become

---

[144] Allen & Boykin
[145] Barbarin
[146] Boykin
[147] Saami et al.

characteristic of the group.

The Gusii, for example, place great importance on suppressing intense emotions, perhaps to maintain harmony in the small living units that are characteristic of that group. In contrast, freedom of emotional expression is, as we all know, consistent with the individualistic approach to life that many mainstream Americans value. We are also aware of psychiatric guidance that encourages the release of emotions. So, we need to remember that not all of the children in our classes will have been brought up in that way.

Cultural influences on emotional behavior can be found in patterns of eye contact. In some African societies, cultural groups believe that eye contact allows another person to inflict harm on the infant. As a result, infants are kept in dark protected environments and are shielded from eye contact when held. The end result is a cool, subdued emotional demeanor. In chapter one we made a connection between poor eye contact and low self-esteem. Does that connection hold true in this instance?

Sometimes cultural practices are based on necessity. Among the Efe people of Central Africa maternal mortality is extremely high. Therefore, infants are often passed from one person to another so that the infant becomes accustomed to multiple caregivers[148]. As a result, infants do not suffer the same sort of emotional stress, described as separation anxiety, that is seen in the West.

Significant numbers of African Americans utilize the power of nurturing to develop self-confidence and self-worth in their children.

---

[148] Saami

In turn, African American children who benefit from this style of parenting become resilient to many distractions in the educational environment that would interfere with focusing on achievement. Caregivers do this by avoiding inflicting their own stresses upon the family unit. When faced with adversity, they find ways to maintain harmony and positive behaviors that will cultivate the resiliency needed by their children in school.

It is argued that nurturance enables caregivers to develop emotional stability in African American children. This stability is then utilized as a resource for academic success in school. On a similar thread, we know that teaching can be a very stressful profession – particularly around exam time. Our students will perform way better if we can shield them from the anxiety and, at times, weariness or disillusion that we might (very temporarily!) be feeling ourselves.

To sum up, significant numbers of black parents across income levels choose practices that they believe will prepare their children for success in school. This preparation includes building resilience to negative social forces that work against success. For example, by combining household structure (i.e., well defined house rules, close supervision, high expectations for children to make responsible choices in and away from home) with high levels of warmth, many African American parents are successful at instilling resilience in their children towards outside pressures and obstacles.

Income

Relations between child rearing and the negatives of marginalization and hardship among low income black families have been well researched. The realities of poverty and unemployment impose an instability upon African American families and as a result can place black children at risk for emotional challenges. Also, higher incidences of debilitating or fatal disease that occur in the black community affect the responsiveness of caregivers[149]. It is suspected that such stressful events, coupled with the ordinary challenges of child rearing, interfere with caregivers' desires to employ the effective listening skills, consistent discipline techniques, problem solving strategies and patience that bringing up children requires. All of these factors affect a child's ability to process and express their own emotions in a healthy way.

Raver states that investigations between low achievement and societal variables – such as poverty – "motivate us to recognize the developmental costs associated with the rising poverty rate among our nation's children". She also believes that research should generate investigations into those processes utilized by caregivers whose children are succeeding against the odds. In the African American community, the caregiver process is best described by approaches are related to contextual and cultural theories that emphasize the role that social connections play in child development.

---

[149] Walker & Singleton

These theories have at their core the pioneering work of Lev Vygotsky[150] and continue to be defined and revised by contemporary researchers.

It's important to realize that these theories differ from those that are prevalent in Western developmental research. The West views individuals as separate from their social and physical environment. This body of research utilizes contextualist and cultural or "socio-cultural" theory as its framework.

It is acknowledged that parenting practices alone will not conquer underachievement in the low-income sector of the black community. Additional tools such as research, public advocacy, and protest are needed to create awareness about the societal barriers that deny access to equal educational opportunities. Such efforts are strengthened, however, by the number of black parents who want their children to go far academically.

---

[150] Luria

Chapter Seven Summary

Key Points

1. Children learn best when their basic needs are being met.
2. Attachment theory emphasizes the child's need to feel safe and secure with an adult.
3. The child's 'attachment figure' provides a safe base from which she can explore the world.
4. Culture influences a black girl's future.
5. Effective parents shield their daughters from stresses they might be experiencing.
6. Poverty can impact emotional resilience.

Reflection Opportunities

- Is your classroom a physically safe environment?
- Is your classroom a psychologically safe environment? Can students feel relaxed and confident about speaking with and in front of their peers?
- Do you consistently implement behavior and anti-bullying policies?
- Are you a calm presence?

8. HER IDENTITY

If you have a culture that determines to an extent your beliefs, your actions, your surroundings then in a way you have a head start on those that don't have that traditional background when it comes to knowing your identity. That's one positive. Another positive is that you have a built-in sense of belonging. But there are rarely ladders without snakes, or swings without roundabouts!

The potential negatives are that it is a shared identity which could become a stereotype; it's an identity that people might attach to you as an African American even when your family identifies more with non-traditional, individualistic approaches.

So how does a black female student find and own her identity?

Cultural Orientation

What is the cultural orientation of black girls, and where does it come from? How does it differ from the mainstream?

Several researchers have elaborated on the notion of a distinct African American culture.

- Shade proposes that African Americans exhibit distinct cognitive styles, that are influenced by a connection to Africa but maintained by the psychological and physical need to survive[151].

- Willis argues that African Americans are strongly influenced by their African heritage and culture, which is characterized by factors of social/affective emphases, harmony, holistic perspectives, expressive creativity, and non-verbal communication[152].

- Nobles describes the self-definition of 'Black America' in terms of an ethos that is shared with most West African tribes: a common will to survive as a people and share in their oneness with nature[153].

- Hale seems to agree with Nobles that "the base of African American culture is West Africa". She identifies certain expressive and behavioral characteristics that link African cultural tradition to contemporary African American culture. These characteristics include song, dance, cooperation and sharing, call and response, spirituality, and emotional expressiveness[154].

- Boykin also claims that the cognition and behavior of black children, termed "Afro culture", comes out of a distinct cultural value system that is rooted in the African American and West African traditions[155].

Whatever best describes the roots of African American identity, the cultural parenting practice of communalism contributes to a black girl's strong sense of herself within the context of her group, family or community and means that her roots will impact on her behavior, likes and dislikes, outcome expectations, self-efficacy, and

---

[151] Shade
[152] Willis
[153] Nobles
[154] Hale-Benson
[155] Allen & Boykin; Boykin; Coleman; Tuck & Boykin

self-esteem: her roots = her identity. This is really important for us, as her educators, to grasp. In an ethnocentric curriculum, room has to be made by us for her to feel motivated by the familiar.

Multiple Identities

There is another way. Other researchers have noted that successful African American parents help their children to develop "multiple identities." For example, Perry reports that successful African American parents teach their children how to live in two worlds. This complicated task requires developing and integrating three identities: (1) a member of mainstream society; (2) a member of a distinct cultural/racial group; and (3) a member of an oppressed group[156].

The African American parents in the above study help their children make sense of these identities in numerous ways. First, parents increase their children's knowledge of their own cultural strengths and historical contributions in an effort to build personal pride. They place a greater emphasis on pride in areas such as racial heritage. In addition, they uphold positive attitudes towards ethnicity, and place importance on social awareness[157].

---

[156] Perry
[157] Bowman & Howard

"The history of the [African American] is the history of this strife – this longing to merge his double self into a better and truer self... In this merging he wishes neither of the older selves to be lost... He simply wishes to make it... possible to be both." W E B DuBois

There is something, I sense, rather sad in that extract from the turn of the last century. A sense that an African American is destined to never be truly "whole." Sadder still that this split between two or more identities has not been resolved in modern America. In a 2016 political article, Chernoh Sesay Jr. writes something very similar. He comments, "writers of African descent who had been the victims of the transatlantic slave trade began to write into existence public black identities. This authorship of identity, community and remembrance took place against a backdrop of tremendous loss – the loss of generations, the loss of ideas, the loss of cultures, the loss of the past, and the loss of the future." He continues: "Rather than an end or outcome in a process of gradual assimilation or cultural loss, black identities are constantly emerging as responses ... the political and cultural identities of black people have never been reducible to a discrete and unified list of interests and ideas.[158]" Ironic, given that a number of researchers have just been cited trying to do exactly that.

Instead of feeling sadness, we can celebrate the fact that African American students have a choice of rich cultures from which to draw. After all, European American literature seems to be built

---

[158] www.aaihs.org/beyond-todays-vote-constructions-of-black-identity-then-and-now

around white crises of identity. An inclusive curriculum (in the face sometimes of centralized directives) can only help all of us to choose who we want to be. You too! Be the teacher you want to be! Encouraging everyone to identify and to reach towards their own strong personal goals.

Chapter Eight Summary

Key Points

1. Black girls have more than one culture to draw their identity (or identities) from: this can have positive and negative consequences.
2. Most African Americans identify most closely with West Africa.
3. Communalism contributes to a black girl's sense of herself.
4. 'Multiple identities' are often encouraged in children by black parents, allowing (or consigning) the child go live in two worlds at the same time.
5. Black girls are encouraged to feel proud about their racial heritage.

Reflection Opportunities

- Do you make it clear to your students through your teaching and resources that no one culture should be prioritized over another?
- Do you teach a subject that lends itself to the exploration of different identities? This could be really helpful if used sensitively. For example, in English class, reading extracts from writers with a range of ethnic backgrounds; or when studying immigration in a humanities subject.
- Are you sure you haven't missed opportunities to celebrate achievements within different cultures?

9. *YOU,* HER TEACHER

Let's begin chapter nine with how we ended chapter eight... you have the power to make a difference in all you students' lives. Now that you've read this book you will feel more confident and informed about how to make a positive difference to the lives of your black female students who, as we have seen, are "at risk" for so many reasons. But you're not superhuman, and we haven't encountered a single researcher who has all the answers. As the research shows, it is mainly African American mothers – and sometimes fathers – who have the greatest impact on their daughters' lives.

Here is what the research says about pedagogy. Afterwards, the next and final chapter summarizes where teachers can affect self-esteem and outcomes in their own classrooms.

Data

Statistical reports investigating the status of African American student achievement continue to show a disparity in academic performance between black and white students. In its report on the educational progress of black students, the National Center for Education Statistics indicated that black students trail white students in areas such as preschool attendance, progress in school, and high school completion. The academic proficiency of African American children is lower than that of their white peers in math, reading, and science. In addition, by age 13, black students are more likely than their white peers to be enrolled in a grade lower than is expected for their age[159].

The African American Education Data Book uses national testing data to show that the majority of African Americans in the 4th, 8th, and 12th grades have not met "basic" levels of achievement in each of the major subject areas. Given such a statistical profile, it is not surprising that a considerable amount of research has been devoted to explaining and raising academic achievement levels of black children.

While academic failings in the African American community continue to be the center of investigations on black student achievement, certain bodies of research have focused on the successes. For example, studies in resilience have identified African American students in low performing communities who are "beating the odds"[160]. These students are performing at or above grade level despite being at risk for academic failure. Brodsky points out that in risk research, positive performance results of students who do not present the same negative outcomes as their low

---

[159] NCES Report 1995
[160] Brodsky

achieving peers are labeled as "false-positives". However, Brodsky argues that high achieving performance outcomes serve to defy negative stereotypes that erroneously define entire communities.

The School Experience

Schools have the responsibility of identifying environmental factors and family practices that facilitate school readiness. Head Start is an example of a school program that utilizes these factors and practices in the classroom and involves parents as well. Programs that assist families in transitioning children from home to school do not exist in every neighborhood. Even for those schools that have transitional programs, the effect of the program does not always carry over into later years.

The ability to develop proficiencies in core curriculum subjects becomes critical as students advance into middle-grade. Lack of access to resources that help older students who are not excelling, such as diagnostic assessments for learning style, learning disabilities (that go beyond the standard and frequently diagnosed attention deficit disorders), and/or effective tutoring, place these students at risk for falling behind. Children experience frustration and despair as learning difficulties go un-addressed. In such cases, teachers are bound to have their attempts to teach these children met with resistance and negative emotions, such as anger, anxiety or sadness. It therefore becomes important for parents and families to be aware of the risk and identify ways that prevent such effects on their children.

Pedagogy – Cultural Integrity

Alternative theories on low academic achievement have focused on student-teacher interaction and culturally relevant pedagogy. One such alternative is the cultural integrity model, which claims that many black students have a distinct system of values, beliefs, and behaviors that are influenced by contemporary African American experiences and fundamental ideologies inherent in the West African tradition.

A significant amount of research suggests that there is a cultural influence on American education that is dominated by mainstream and middle-class values. It is argued that this cultural dominance creates a hegemonic environment that disenfranchises children who approach learning with differing cultural orientations[161]. Boykin argues that "there is a profound, cultural fabric to the schooling process in America", which is interlocked with mainstream characteristics that are viewed favorably in other institutions in the larger society[162].

In other words, the curriculum reflects the white ethnocentric society that governs America as a whole. This cultural fabric, which

---

[161] Erickson; Davis; Davis and Golden; Walton
[162] Boykin

was openly promoted during the initial implementation of public education[163], has evolved into the foundation upon which schooling institutions are built. Current educational practices exude an expectation of mainstream cultural behavior that is assumed to be universal, "correct" and "civilized"[164].

When considering culture and schooling, a distinction should be made between culture at the "surface" structure level versus culture at a "deep" structure level[165].

Culture at the surface structure level highlights the need for the pedagogical inclusion of categories including cultural history, positive cultural images, and contributions of people of color[166]. Attention to this area can be found in research on the black student experience and multiculturalism[167]. While culture at this level is needed in order to "reverse the effects of rendering black children emotionally and spiritually invisible"[168], culture in the classroom must penetrate further.

Culture at the deep structure level is understood in terms of how a group of people codifies reality. It is the fundamental bases for life prescription, or life rules of a people. Culture at the level of deep structure encompasses fundamental ideals, beliefs, and values of a people that give direction to their lives and to their group creation[169]. It is culture at this level that embodies the essence of

---

[163] Vallence
[164] Boykin
[165] Ibid.
[166] Henry
[167] Davis; Merrelman
[168] Ibid.
[169] Boykin; Ani

black children's life experiences, and it will need to be accessed before schools can expect to see the positive effects of employing black culture in the classroom on academic achievement. Additional research describes how classroom practices of mainstream culture at the level of deep structure empower some children and place others at a disadvantage.

Gender

Discrepancies in academic achievement among African American adolescents have been widely examined and as a result many researchers have suggested a need to further study what they speculate is a gendered racial culture among these students. For example, researchers suggest that African American adolescents function in a climate where teachers favor females over males. This could contribute to the achievement gap between the African American female and the male.

Greene & DeBacker examined gender differences and academic achievement and produced mixed results. These authors suggest in earlier studies that females set fewer short-term goals and are more pessimistic about their goals than males. Together with others they then suggested that contributing factors to the pessimistic view of the future among females was the expectation of negotiating more life transition than males and having to place on hold their future academic and career goals for marriage and family [170].

Curriculum

Evidence suggest that African American parents desire schools to place a greater emphasis on African American heritage. Although they believe the school's curriculum should incorporate the historical contributions of African Americans, they distrust schools' commitment to equality or equity and believe the school systems are ill-equipped to do an adequate job if allowed to assume this responsibility[171].

On the other hand, and this ties in with observations on multi-identities in the preceding chapter, these parents help their children understand the dominant culture's values, manners, history, and expectations in order for their children to be viewed by school personnel as ready to learn.

---

[170] Nurmi; Greene & Wheatly; Trommsdorff
[171] Perry

Chapter Nine Summary

Key Points

1. You *can* make a difference.
2. Black students have a tendency to fall behind white students in terms of academic progress.
3. Be aware of environmental factors and family practices impacting on your black female students' readiness to learn.
4. Make use of diagnostic tests where appropriate through close liaison with learning support staff.
5. Black poverty can affect access to school resources.
6. Cultural integrity suggests that you should attempt to make your lessons less traditionally ethnocentric.
7. White cultural dominance disenfranchises black students.
8. Culture can be defined at both a 'surface' and 'deep' level.

Reflection Opportunities

- When did you last make a difference to a black girl's self-esteem?
- Who can you make a difference to today?

Senior Teachers' Checklist

Key Questions to Ask at a Recruitment Interview

- Based on any research you might be aware of on black girls' progress, how will you prepare them for success on the standardized assessments?
- How do you make sure you meet the needs of black girls with low self-esteem?
- How might you communicate differently with the parents of black girls (if at all)?
- Describe your philosophy with regard to multiracial / multicultural education?
- Do you know anything about the history of 'at-risk' black girls in public schools?
- Why might some female students of color be lacking in self-esteem?
- How can you make the curriculum appeal to students of all races and cultures?
- If you were in government, is there anything you would change about the curriculum to help reduce feelings of marginalization among specific groups?
- Can you tell me about a recent lesson where you used resources or subject matter that were African in origin? Eg. a black writer, scientist, artist, black history.
- Does the ethnicity of your students affect your lesson- planning? Why?
- How do you ensure your classroom is a safe environment for everybody?
- How would you deal with a racist incident in your classroom / corridor / recess social area?
- How do you define racism?
- Explain to me why your classroom is 'inclusive'.
- Think of one thing you could do to make your classroom more inclusive to female African American students.

AFTERWORD

Whether you have chosen to read every word of this guide to teaching at-risk African American schoolgirls, or focused on one chapter, or simply made note of the nine checklists, it is my hope that it is a book to which you will return again and again and recommend to other educators. I'd love it if you used it as a working document – adding to it your own notes and observations as you go along year on year.

My overwhelming hope that is that as society progresses (which can only happen if people like you, people who have chosen to find out about 'the other' in an effort to be more inclusive and fair), we will one day reach a point where no culture dominates our classrooms, where all students – all races, both sexes – feel empowered and valued and no longer burdened by economic or racial inequalities. Where fathers and father figures are expected to multitask no less than the female caregivers and enjoy doing so too! Where families can take the shape that works best for them without fear of stigma or marginalization.

In the meantime, let's work hard as dedicated and passionate teaching professionals to make as much positive difference to the lives of those in our classrooms as we can.

BIBLIOGRAPHY/REFERENCES

Abel, Y. (2012). African American fathers' involvement in their children's school-based lives. The Journal of Negro Education, 81(2), 162-172.

Adams, C.J. (2005). Poor African American fathers: An evolutionary perspective. Journal of Infant, Child, and Adolescent Psychotherapy, 4(4), 378-407.

Ahmeduzzaman, M., & Roopnarine, J. (1992). Sociodemographic factors, functioning style, social support, and fathers; invovlement with preschoolers in African-American families. Journal of Marriage and the Family,54, 699-707.

Albert, K.A., & Luzzo, D.A. (1999). The role of perceived barriers in career development: A social cognitive perspective. Journal of Counseling and Development, 77(4), 431- 436.

Allen, S., & Daly, K. (2007). The effects of father involvement:An updated research summary of evidence. Father Involvement Research Alliance, 1-53.

Allgood,S.M., Beckert, T.E., & Peterson, C. (2012). The role of father involvement in the perceived psychological well-being of young adult daughters: A retrospective study. North American Journal of Psychology, 14(1), 95-110.

Alliman-Brissett, A.E., Turner, S.L.,& Skovholt, T.M. (2004). Parent support and African American adolescents' career self-efficacy. Professional School Counseling,7, 124-132.

Anderson, E. A., Kohler, J. K., & Letiecq, B. L. (2005). Predictors of depression among low-income, nonresidential fathers. Journal of Family Issues, 26, 547-567.

Arnold, D.H., Zeljo, A., Doctoroff, G.L., Ortiz, C. (2008). Parent involvement in preschool; Predictors nad the relation of involvement to preliteracy development. School Psychology Review, 37(1), 74-90.

Baldwin, K.M., Baldwin, J.R., & Ewald, T. (2006). The relationship among shame, guilt, and self-efficacy. American Journal of Psychotherapy, 60(1), 1- 21.

Bandura, A. (1986). Social foundations of thought and action: A social cognitive theory. Engelwood Cliffs. NJ: Prentice Hall.

Bandura, A. (1997). Self-efficacy: The exercise of control. New York: Freeman.

Banerjee, M., Harrell, Z.A.T., & Johnson, D.J. (2011). Racial/ethnic socialization and parental involvement in education as predictors of cognitive ability and achievement in African American children. Journal of Youth Adolescence, 40, 595-605.

Baytop, C. M. (2006). Evaluating the effectiveness of programs to improve educational attainment of unwed African American teen mothers: A meta analysis. The Journal of Negro Education, 75(3), 458-477.

Bettmann, J.E. (2006). Using attachment theory to understand the treatment of adult depression. Clinical Social Work Journal, 34(4), 531-542.

Bloom, M., Fischer, J., & Orme, J.G. (2006). Evaluating practice: Guidelines for the accountable professional (5th ed.). Boston, MA: Pearson.

Boatwright, K. J., & Egidio, R. K. (2003). Psychological predictors of college women's leadership aspirations. Journal of College Student Development, 44(5), 653-669.

Booth, C.S., & Myers, J.E. (2011). Differences in career and life planning between African American and Caucasian undergraduate women. Journal of Multicultural Counseling and Development, 39(1), 14- 23.

Bronte-Tinkew, J., Scott, M. E., & Lilja, E. (2010). Single custodial fathers' involvement and parenting: Implications for outcomes in emerging adulthood. Journal of Marriage and Family, 72(5), 1107-1127.

Brown, T.L., Linver, M.R., Evans, M., & DeGennaro, D. (2009). African American parents' racial and ethnic socialization and adolescent academic grades: Testing out the role of gender. Journal of Youth and Adolescent, 38, 214-227.

Bryant, A.L., & Zimmerman, M.A. (2003). Role models and psychosocial outcomes among African American adolescents. Journal of Adolescent Research, 18, 36-67.

Buchanan, N.T, & Ormerod, A.J. (2002). Racialized sexual harassment in the lives of African American women. Women & Therapy, 25(3/4), 107-125.

Byars, A.M. (2001). Rights of way: Affirmative career counseling with African American women. In W.B. Walsh, R.P. Bingham, M.T. Brown, & C.M. Ward (Eds.), Career counseling for African Americans (pp,113-137). Mahwah, NJ: Erlbaum.

Byars, A.M., & Hackett, G. (1998). Applications of social cognitive theory to the career development of women of color. Applied & Preventive Psychology, 7, 255-267.

Carson, L. R. (2009). "I am because we are:" collectivism as a foundational characteristic of African American college student identity and academic achievement. Social Psychology of Education : An International Journal, 12(3), 327-344.

Chabris, C., & Simons, D. (2010). The invisible gorilla: and other ways our intuition deceive us. New York: Crown.

Chadiha, L. A., Adams, P., Biegel, D. E., Auslander, W., & Gutierrez, L. (2004). Empowering African American women informal caregivers: A literature synthesis and practice strategies. Social Work, 49(1), 97-108.

Cheatham, H.E. (1990). Africentricity and career development. The Career Development Quarterly, 38, 334-346.

Choi, J., & Jackson, A. P. (2012). Nonresident fathers' parenting, maternal mastery and child development in poor African American single-mother families. Race and Social Problems, 4(2), 102-111.

Chronister, K.M. & McWhirter, E.H. (2003). Applying Social cognitive career theory to the empowerment of battered women. Journal of Counseling & Development. 81, 418-425.

Clayton, O., Mincy, R. B., & Blankenhorn, D. (Eds.). (2006). Fatherhood. Black fathers in contemporary American society: strengths, weaknesses, and strategies for change. New York, NY: Russell Sage.

Cochran, D.L. (1997). African American fathers: A decade review of the literature. The Journal of Contemporary Human Services 78(4), 340-351.

Cohen, J. (1992). A power primer. Psychological Bulletin, 112(1), 155-159.

Coley, R. L. (2003). Daughter-father relationships and adolescent psychosocial functioning in low-income African American families. Journal of Marriage and Family, 65, 867-875.

Coley, R.L. (2003). Daughter-father relationships and adolescent psychological functioning in low-income African American families. Journal of Marriage and Family, 65, 867-875.

Coltrane, S. (2006). Fathering: paradoxes, contradictions and dilemmas. Handbook of contemporary families, 46-64.

Combs, G. N. (2003). The duality of race and gender for managerial African American women: Implications of informal social networks on career advancement. Human Resource Development Review, 2(4), 385-405.

Connor, M. E., & White, J. L. (Eds.). (2011). Preface. Black fathers an invisible presence in America (2 ed., pp. 1-257). New York, NY: Routledge Taylor & Francis.

Cooper, S.M. (2009). Associations between father-daughter relationship quality and the academic engagement of African American adolescent girls: Self-esteem as a mediator? Journal of Black Psychology, 35(4), 495-516.

Creamer, E.G., & Laughlin, A. (2005). Self-authorship and women's career decision making. Journal of College Student Development, 46, 13-27.

Creswell, J. W. (2009). Research design: Qualitative, quantitative, and mixed methods approaches (3rd ed.). Thousand Oaks, CA: Sage.

Cron, E.A. (2001). Job satisfaction in dual-career women at three family life cycle stages. Journal of Career Development, 28(1), 17-28.

Crowley, J. E., & Curenton, S. (2011). Organizational social support and parenting challenges among mothers of color: The case of mocha moms. Family Relations, 60(1), 1-14.

Curry, C., Trew, K., Turner, I., & Hunter, J. (1994). The effect of life domains on girls' possible selves. Adolescence, 29, 133-150.

Davis, G.R. (2012). Exploring the relationship between African American father involvement and the academic success of their college –age children.(Doctoral Dissertation).

DeVaney, S.B., & Hughey, A.W. (2000). Career development of ethnic minority students. In D.A. Luzzo (ed.), Career counseling of college students: An empirical guide to strategies that work (pp.233-252). Washington, DC: American Psychological Association.

Douglas, W. (2003). Television families: Is something wrong in suburbia. Mahweh,NJ: Routledge.

Dubowitz, H., Lane ,W., Greif, G.L., Jenson, T.K., & Lamb, M.E. (2006). Low-income African American fathers' involvement in children's lives: Implications for practitioners. Journal of Family Social Work, 10(1), 25-41

Dufur, J. (2010, September 29). Sex differences in parenting in single mother and single father households. Journal of marriage and family, 72, 1092-1106.

Earl, L., & Lohmann, N. (1978). Absent fathers and black male children. Social Work, 23, 413-415.

Eisenberg, N., & Lennon, R. (1983). Sex differences in empathy. Psychological Bullentin, 94, 100-131.

Eshleman, J. R., & Bulcroft, R. A. (2010). The family (12th ed.). Boston: Allyn & Bacon.

Fagan, J. (1996). Principles for developing male involvement programs in early childhood setting: personal experience. Young Children, 51, 64-71.

Finley, G.E. & Schwartz, S.J. (2004). The father involvement and nurturant fathering scales: Retrospective measures for adolescents and adult children. Educational and Psychological Measurement, 64(1), 143-164.

Flouri, E., Buchanan, A., & Bream, V. (2002). Adolescents" perception of their fathers' involvement: Significance to school attitudes. Psychology in the Schools, 39, 575-582.

Fouad, N., & Byars-Winston, A. (2005). Cultural context of career choice: Meta-analysis of race/ethnicity differences. The Career

Development Quarterly, 53, 223-233.

Greene, B. A., & DeBacker, T. K. (2004). Gender and orientations toward the future: Links to motivation. Educational Psychology Review, 16(2), 91-120.

Greene, J. (2003). Sadistic statistics: Part II. Correlations. In Glicken, M.D. (Ed.). Social research: A simple guide. Boston, MA: Pearson.

Greer, T.M., & Brown, P. (2011). Minority status stress and coping processes among African American college students. Journal of Diversity in Higher Education, 4(1), 26-38.

Hackett, G. & Byars, A.M. (1996). Social cognitive theory and career development of African American women. The Career Development Quarterly, 44(4), 322-340.

Hamer, J. (1998). What African-American noncustodial father says inhibits and enhances their involvement with children. Western Journal of Black Studies, 22, 117-127.

Hamer, J. F. (2001). What does it mean to be daddy? New York, Chichester, West Sussex: Columbia University Press.

Hamer, J., & Marchioro, K. (2002). Becoming custodial dads: Exploring parenting among low-income and working-class African American fathers. Journal of Marriage and Family, 64(1), 116-129.

Hammond, W.P., Caldwald, C.H.,Brooks, C., & Bell,L. (2011). Being there in spirit, fire, and, mind: Expressive roles among nonresidential African American fathers. Research on Social Work Practice, 21(3), 308-318.

Hanson, S. (2007). Success in science among young African American women: The role of minority families. Journal of Family Issues, 28, 3-33.

Helwig, A.A. (2008). From childhood to adulthood: A 15-year

longitudinal development study. The Career Development Quarterly, 57 (1), 38-50.

Herring, C., & Wilson-Sadberry, K.R. (1993). Preference or necessity? Changing work roles of Black and White women, 1973-1990. Journal of Marriage and the Family, 55, 314-325.

Hill, N.E., Castellino, D.R., Lansford, J.E., Nowlin, P., Dodge, K.A., Bates, J.E., & Pettit, G.S. (2004). Parent academic involvement as related to school behavior, achievement, and aspirations. Child Development, 75(5), 1491-1509.

Hill, S. A. (2006). Marriage among African American women: A gender perspective. Journal of Comparative Family Studies, 37(3), 421-III.

Hines, A. (1997). Divorce-related transitions, adolescent development, and the role of the parent-child relationship: A review of the literature. Journal of Marriage and Family, 59(2), 375- 388.

Hite, L. M., & McDonald, K. S. (2003). Career aspirations of non-managerial women: Adjustment and adaptation. Journal of Career Development, 29(4), 221-235.

Holland, J. L., & Gottfredson, G. (1994). Career attitudes and strategies inventory: An inventory for understanding adult careers. Mental Measurements Yearbook with Tests in Print.

Hollinger, C.L. (1991). Facilitating the career development of gifted young women. Roeper Review, 13, 135-139.

Honora, D. T. (2002). The relationship of gender and achievement to future outlook among African American adolescents. Adolescence, 37(146), 301-316.

Horn, P. (1995). Children's work and welfare, 1780-1890. Cambridge University: Cambridge University Press.

Jacobs, E. E., Masson, R.L. & Harvill, R. L. (2009). Group counseling: Strategies and skills. (6th ed.). Belmont, CA: Thomson learning.

Kerpelman, J.L., & Schvaneveldt, P.L. (1999). Young adults' anticipated identity commitments to career, marital, and parental roles: Comparisons of men and women with different role balance orientations. Sex Roles, 41, 189-217.

Kerpelman, J.L., Eryigit, S., & Stephens, C.J. (2007). African American adolescents' future education orientation: Associations with self-efficacy, ethnic identity, and perceived parental support. J Youth Adolescence, 37, 997-1008.

King, V., Harris, K.M., & Heard, H.E. (2004). Racial and ethnic diversity in nonresident father involvement. Journal of Marriage and Family, 66, 1-21.

Klonoff, E.A., Landrine, H. (1999). Cross-validation of the schedule of racist events. Journal of African American Psychology, 25, 231-254.

Leaper, C., Farkas, T., & Brown, C. S. (2012). Adolescent girls' experiences and gender-related beliefs in relation to their motivation in math/science and English. Journal of youth and adolescence, 41(3), 268-282.

Leavell, A. S., Tamis-lemonda, C., Ruble, D. N., Zosuls, K. M., & Cabrera, N. J. (2012). African American, White and Latino fathers' activities with their sons and daughters in early childhood. Sex Roles, 66(1-2), 53-65.

Lemish, D. (2007). Children and Television: A global perspective by Dafna Lemish. Malden, MA: Blackwell .

Lent, R. W., Brown, S.D., & Hackett, G. (1994). Toward a unifying socia cognitive theory of career and academic interst, choice, and performance. Journal of Vocational Behavior, 45, 79-122.

Lent, R.W., & Brown, S.D. (1996). Social cognitive approach to career development: An overview. The Career Development Quarterly, 44, 310-321.

Lerman, R. I. (Ed.). (1993). Evolution of unwed fatherhood as a policy issue. Young unwed fathers changing roles and emerging policies (pp. 1-335). Temple University: Temple University Press.

Levine, K. A., & Sutherland, D. (2013). History repeats itself: Parental involvement in children's career Exploration/L'histoire se répète : La participation des parents dans l'exploration de carrière pour enfants. Canadian Journal of Counselling and Psychotherapy, 47(2), 239-255.

Li, C., & Kerpelman, J.L. (2007). Parental influences on youmg women's certainty about their career aspirations. Sex Roles, 56, 105-115.

Mandara, J., Murray, C. B., Telesford, J. M., Varner, F. A., & Richman, S. B. (2012). Observed gender differences in African American mother-child relationships and child behavior. Family Relations, 61(1), 129-141.

Marbley, A. F. (2005). African-American women's feelings on alienation from third-wave feminism: A conversation with my sisters. Western Journal of Black Studies, 29(3), 605-614.
Marion, M. S., & Range, L. M. (2003). African American college women's suicide buffers. Suicide & Life - Threatening Behavior, 33(1), 33-43.

McBride, B. A., & Rane, T. R. (1997). Father/Male involvement in early childhood programs: issues and challenges. Early Childhood Education Journal, 25, 11-15.

McBride, B.A., Schoppe-Sullivan, S.J., & Ho, M.H. (2005). The mediating role of fathers' school involvement on students' achievement. Applied Developmental Psychology, 26, 201-216.

McClain, L. R., P.H.D., & DeMaris, A., P.H.D. (2013). A better deal for cohabitating fathers? Union status difference in father involvement. Fathering, 11(2), 199-220.

Morgan, S., & Morgan, M. (2001). Father -Daughter: contemporary research and issues. Mahweh, NJ: Routledge Taylor& Francis

Group.

Mori, M. (1990). The influence of father-daughter relationship and girls; sex-role on girls' self-esteem. Archives of Women's Mental Health, 2(1), 45-47.

Mori, M. (1998). The Influence of father-daughter relationship on girls' self-esteem. Archives of Women's Mental Health, 2, 45.

National Institute of Health: The Department of Bioethics. (2012). Research involving vunerable populations.

Nawaz, S., & Gilani, N. (2011). Relationship of parental and peer attachment bonds with career decision-making self-efficacy among adolescents and post-adolescents. Journal of Behavioural Sciences, 21(1), 33-47.

Neal, D. (2004). The measured Black-White wage gap among women is too small. Journal of Political Economy, 112(1), 1-28.

Nielsen, L. (2012). Father daughter relationships Contemporary research and issues. New York, NY: Routledge Taylor& Francis Group.

Nurmi, J.E., Seginer, R., & Poole, M. (1990). The future education orientation questionnaire. Helsinki, Finland: University of Helsinki, Department of Psychology.

Osarenren, N., Nwadinigwe, P., & Awazie, E. (2013). Effect of Fathering methods and child environmental factors on adolescents vulnerability to delinquency in Mushin area of Lagos, Nigeria. British Journal of Arts and Social Sciences, 12, 127-142.
Paa, H. K., & McWhirter, E.H. (2000). Perceived influences on high school students' current career expectations. The Career Development Quarterly, 49(1), 29-44.

Palkovitz, R. (2002). Men's construction of the fathering role: balancing the demands of what it means to be a dad today. In Involved fathering and men's adult development: provisional balances (pp. 1-307). Mahwah, NJ: Lawrence Erlbaum.

Parham, T., & Austin, N.L. (1994). Career development and African Americans : A contextual reappraisal using the nigrescence construct. Journal of Vocational Behavior, 44, 139-154.

Patrick, P. K. S. (2007). Contemporary issues in counseling. Boston: Allyn & Bacon.

Pearson, S.M., & Bieschke, K.J. (2001). Succeeding againist the odds: An examination of familial influences on the career development of professional African American women. Journal of Counseling Psychology, 48(3), 301-309.

Percheski, C. (2008). Opting out? cohort differences in professional women's employment rates from 1960 to 2005. American Sociological Review, 73(3), 497-517.

Perrone, K.M, Webb, L.K, & Jackson, Z.V. (2007). Relationships between parental attachment, work and family roles, and life satisfaction. The Career Development Quarterly, 55(3), 237-248.

Pleck, E. H., & Pleck, J. H. (1997). Fatherhood ideals in the United States: Historical dimensions"(3 ed.). Hillsdale, NJ: Lawrence Erlbaum.

Powell, K. C. (2004). Developmental Psychology of Adolescent Girls: Conflicts and Identity Issues. Education, 125(1), 77.
Ramanathan, M. (2006). Ethics in quantitative research methods. Retrieved   from http://icmr.nic.in/bioethics/cc_biothics/presentations/haryana/session61.pdf

Renfro-Michel, E.L., Burlew, L.D., & Robert, T. (2009). The interaction of work adjustment and attachment theory: Employment counseling implications. Journal of Employment Counseling, 46, 18-26.

Roberts, R.E., Phinney, J.S., Masse, L.C., Chen Y.R., Roberts, C. R.,

& Romero, A. (1999). The structure of ethnic identity of young adolescents from diverse ethno cultural groups. Journal of Early Adolescence, 19, 301-322.

Robinson, T. N., Killen, J. D., Kraemer, H. C., Wilson, D. M., Matheson, D. M., Haskell, W. L., ... & Varady, A. (2003). Dance and reducing television viewing to prevent weight gain in African-American girls: the Stanford GEMS pilot study.Ethnicity and Disease, 13(1; SUPP/1), S1-65.

Rogers, M.A., Theule, J., Ryan, B.A., Adams, G.R., & Keating, L. (2009). Parental involvement and children's school achievement. Canadian Journal of School Psychology, 24(1), 34-57.

Ruiz, D. S. (2008). The changing roles of African American grandmothers raising grandchildren: An exploratory study in the piedmont region of North Carolina. Western Journal of Black Studies, 32(1), 62-71.

Russell, E.R. (2005). Career activities and worldview: Impact of an intervention using the Career Attitudes and Strategies Inventory (Doctoral Dissertation). Retrieved from ProQuest Dissertations and Theses database. (UMI No. 3184885)

Salem, D.A., Zimmerman, M.A., & Notaro, P.C. (1998). Effects of family structure, family process, and father involvement on psychological outcomes among African American adolescents. Family Relations, 47,331-341.

Sherer, M., Maddux, J., Mercandante, B., Prentice-Dunn, S., Jacobs, B., & Rogers, R. (1982). The self-efficacy scale: Construction and validation. Psychological Review, 51, 663-671.

Smith, C. A., Krohn, M. D., Chu, R., & Best, O. (2005). African American fathers: Myths and realities about their involvement with their firstborn children. Journal of Family Issues, 26, 975-1001.

Spera, C., Wentzel, K. R., & Matto, H. C. (2009). Parental aspirations for their children's educational attainment: Relations to ethnicity, parental education, children's academic performance, and parental perceptions of school climate. Journal of Youth and Adolescence, 38(8), 1140-52.

Stetz, M. (2007). Hollywood fathers and daughters. Literature and Film Quarterly, 35, 116-132.

Szymanski, D.M., & Stewart, D.N. (2010). Racism and sexism as correlates of African American women's psychological distress. Sex Roles, 63, 226-238.

Theran, S. A. (2009). Predictors of level of voice in adolescent girls: Ethnicity, attachment, and gender role socialization. Journal of Youth and Adolescence, 38(8), 1027-1037.

Thomas, D. M., Love, K. M., Roan-Belle, C., Tyler, K. M., Brown, C. L., & Garriott, P. O. (2009). Self-efficacy, motivation, and academic adjustment among African American women attending institutions of higher education. The Journal of Negro Education, 78(2), 159-171.

Thomas, P. A., Krampe, E. M., & Newton, R. R. (2008). Father presence, family structure, and feelings of closeness to the father among adult African American children. Journal of Black Studies, 529-546.

Thomas, P.A., Krampe, E.M., & Newton, R.R. (2008). Father presence, family structure, and feelings of closeness to the father among adult African American children. Journal of Black Studies, 38(4), 529-546.

Trescott, J. (1995). While the plight of young males tops the black agenda, girls face crises of lost self-esteem and dreams. Emerge, 6.

Tripp-Reissman, T., & Wilson, S. E. (1990). Cross-cultural perspective on fatherhood. In Daddy fatherhood for black men living away from their children. Chi Chester, West Sussex, NY: Columbia University Press.

Troilo, J., & Coleman, M. (2008). College student perceptions of the content of father stereotypes. JMF, 70(1), 218-227.

Trotman, M.F. (2001). Involving the African American parent: Recommendations to increase the level of parent involvement within African American families. The Journal of Negro Education, 70(4), 275-285.

Trusty, J. (2002). African American's educational expectations: Longitudinal causal models for women and men. Journal of Counseling and Development : JCD, 80(3), 332-345.

Vazsonyi, A.T., Hibbert, J.R., & Snider, J.B. (2003). Exotic enterprise no more? Adolescent reports of family and parenting processes from youth in four countries. Journal of Research on Adolescence, 13, 129-160.

Watson, C. M., Quatman, T., & Edler, E. (2002). Career aspirations of adolescent girls: Effects of achievement level, grade, and single- sex school environment. Sex Roles, 46(9), 323-335.

White, A. M. (2006). African American feminist fathers' narratives of parenting. Journal of Black Psychology, 32, 43-51.

Wiemann, C., Agurcia, C., Rickert, V., Berenson, A., & Volt, R. (2006). Absent fathers as providers: race/ethnic differences in support for adolescent mothers. Child & Adolescent Social Work Journal, 23, 617-634.

Williams, C.B., & Wiggins, M.I. (2010). Womanist spirituality as a response to the racism-sexism double bind in African American women. Counseling and Values, 54, 175-186.

Zimmerman, M.A., Salem, D.A., & Maton, K.I. (1995). Family structure and psychosocial correlates among urban African American adolescent males. Child Development, 66, 1598-1613.

Zunker, V. G. (2006). Career counseling: A holistic approach. (7th ed.). Belmont, CA: Brooks/Cole.

ABOUT THE AUTHOR

Theodore was born in Dallas, Texas to Drinkard and Lonnie Timms. He has two older brothers, Michael and Drinkard Jr, and a sister, Tanya. Drinkard Jr. recently passed away.

His father was an A.M.E. preacher who was the pastor of several churches throughout the state of Texas which forced him to enroll in several different schools throughout his elementary. This deeply affected him academically. He was always 'playing catchup'.

He finally settled in San Antonio, where he finished middle and high school. He then wanted to attend college, but a few people said he was 'not college material'. Harsh, but he says that 'they were partially correct. I graduated from high school in the bottom of my class with a 1.71. I did not tell anyone, not even my parents, because I was embarrassed'.

Most people would have given up but with grit and agency he graduated from the University of North Texas with a BS in Education and from Texas A & M University-Commerce with an M.Ed. He went on to receive numerous awards for his teaching, and for the schools at which he taught was a senior manager.

He was accepted into the university's doctoral program but did not finish because he was advised to change his topic - and refused to do so, given the importance of the subject. His dissertation has instead evolved into this book you are now holding.

Made in the USA
Monee, IL
02 September 2023

41990097R10080